Revolutionizing Law Enforcement

Cold Case Investigations Through

DNA Genealogy

Solving The Unsolvable Through Genetic

Detective Work

Revolutionizing Law Enforcement Cold Case Investigations Through DNA Genealogy

Solving The Unsolvable Through Genetic Detective Work

By

(James E. Lefemine)

This is a work of creative nonfiction. Some parts have been fictionalized in varying degrees for various purposes.

James E. Lefemine

COPYRIGHT

DISCLAIMER

This guide is intended for information and educational purposes only. In no event shall its authors, publishers, suppliers or partners be liable for any damages (including without limitation, damages for loss of data or profit, or due to business interruption) arising out of the use or inability to use the materials in this guide. Readers are advised to conduct their own research and due diligence and consult with a qualified professional before making any purchasing or financial decisions.

DISCLOSURE

This electronic version of this book may include hyperlinks to products and learning resources for reader convenience. The authors participate in various affiliate programs which may cover some of the tools and resources mentioned in this guide. This means they may earn a nominal fee on purchases from related partner websites.

About the Author

James E. Lefemine, known affectionately as Jim to his friends, is a dedicated family man and passionate historian. Jim has a BA from the University of South Florida, where he immersed himself in a blend of the Social Sciences. Married with two children and three grandchildren, Jim's interest in genealogy was sparked by the expansion of his own family, revealing a rich tapestry of ancestral stories.

Since taking on the role of family historian in 2014, Jim has delved deep into his roots, meticulously researching and constructing a family tree that now boasts over 2,900 ancestors spanning more than 1,500 years. This journey into his past has become a labor of love, with Jim dedicating many hours each month to further expanding his knowledge of his family's history.

Jim's passion for history extends beyond his own lineage. While researching family members who served in World War II, he became involved in broader historical projects. In 2014, he served as the Historical Researcher for "Red Tracers," the WWII

Unit History Book of the 482nd AAA Battalion, written by Walt Cross.

Drawing on his father's military experiences, Jim authored and edited two books about WWII air combat units. The first, "319th Heavy Bombardment Squadron of the 90th Bombardment Group in the South-West Pacific," was re-published on September 20, 2014. His second work, "The Black Pirates: 400th Bomb Squadron in the Southwest Pacific, 1942-1944: The Jolly Rogers 400th Bomb Squadron Unit History," followed shortly after, published on October 17, 2014.

Continuing Jim's passion for all things family history, Jim published 2 books; Roots And Branches: A Guide To Building Your Family Genealogy Tree and also it's sequel, Roots And Branches II: A Guide To DNA Genealogy To Help Build Your Family Tree.

Today, Jim continues his passionate work in genealogical research, driven by his curiosity about his family's past. This has allowed Jim to explore other areas where genealogy, including DNA genealogy have impacted social science, including police investigative work solving cold case crimes.

Table of Contents

Part I: Foundations

Chapter 1: The Evolution of DNA in Criminal Investigations

I. Historical Perspective on DNA Evidence

The history of DNA evidence in criminal investigations reflects a fascinating journey of scientific discovery, technological advancement, and its gradual integration into the justice system. Deoxyribonucleic acid (DNA), the molecule carrying genetic information in nearly all living organisms, has revolutionized the way crimes are solved, offering unmatched precision in identifying individuals. However, the use of DNA in forensic science is a relatively recent development, with its origins dating back to the latter half of the 20th century.

The Discovery of DNA and Its Structure

DNA was first identified in 1869 by Swiss biochemist Friedrich Miescher, who isolated a substance from the nuclei of white blood cells that he called "nuclein." Though its significance was not understood at the time, this discovery laid the foundation for further research. Decades later, in 1953, James Watson and Francis Crick famously uncovered the double-helix structure of DNA, a breakthrough that revealed how genetic information is stored and replicated.

Despite this foundational knowledge, it took several decades before the practical application of DNA in identifying individuals became possible. Early DNA research focused on understanding genetics, heredity, and biological processes, with no immediate connection to criminal investigations. However, as scientists developed methods to analyze DNA sequences, the potential for its use in forensic science became apparent.

DNA Evidence Enters the Forensic Landscape

The first major leap in DNA's application to criminal investigations came in 1984, when Dr. Alec Jeffreys, a British geneticist, discovered DNA fingerprinting. Jeffreys found that certain regions of DNA contained sequences that varied greatly among individuals, making them unique identifiers. This discovery revolutionized the field of forensic science, providing a new tool for solving crimes that had previously relied heavily on circumstantial evidence or less precise identification methods like fingerprinting.

The first criminal case involving DNA evidence occurred in 1986 in the United Kingdom. Police were investigating the rape and murder of two teenage girls in Narborough, Leicestershire. Initially, a suspect named Richard Buckland had confessed to one of the murders, but investigators sought to confirm his involvement using the new DNA profiling technique. Jeffreys compared DNA samples from the crime scene to Buckland's DNA and found no match, exonerating him. Subsequently, a mass DNA screening of local men led to the identification of Colin Pitchfork as the perpetrator. Pitchfork's conviction marked the first time DNA evidence was used to both clear an innocent suspect and secure a guilty verdict.

Growth and Acceptance of DNA Evidence

Following the Pitchfork case, DNA evidence rapidly gained acceptance in criminal justice systems worldwide. In the late 1980s and early 1990s, advances in polymerase chain reaction (PCR) technology enabled scientists to amplify small amounts of DNA, making it possible to analyze degraded or minute samples. This technological leap significantly expanded the utility of DNA in solving crimes.

By the 1990s, DNA databases were established to store genetic profiles of offenders, facilitating the rapid comparison of DNA evidence from crime scenes with known profiles. The United Kingdom launched the National DNA Database (NDNAD) in 1995, becoming a model for other countries. In the United States, the Combined DNA Index System (CODIS) was introduced, allowing law enforcement agencies to share and search DNA profiles across jurisdictions.

Early Challenges and Criticism

Despite its promise, DNA evidence faced skepticism in its early years. Defense attorneys often challenged its reliability, arguing that laboratory errors or contamination could lead to false results. Courts grappled with questions about the admissibility of DNA evidence, particularly concerning the validity of statistical probabilities used to convey the likelihood of a match. High-profile cases, such as the 1995 trial of O.J. Simpson, brought these debates into the public spotlight, highlighting both the power and potential pitfalls of DNA technology.

In addition to legal challenges, early DNA testing was time-consuming and expensive, limiting its accessibility to high-profile cases. Forensic laboratories lacked the capacity to handle large caseloads, and the backlog of unprocessed samples became a significant issue.

II.   Limitations of Traditional DNA Matching

While traditional DNA matching has been a groundbreaking tool for solving crimes, it is not without limitations. These constraints have shaped the evolution of forensic science and underscore the need for complementary technologies, such as genetic genealogy, to address unresolved challenges.

1. Dependency on Quality and Quantity of DNA Samples

Traditional DNA matching requires high-quality and sufficient quantities of DNA to produce reliable results. In many criminal investigations, the available DNA evidence may be degraded due to exposure to environmental factors such as heat, moisture, or sunlight. For instance, in cold cases where evidence has been stored for decades, DNA samples are often fragmented or contaminated, rendering them unsuitable for standard analysis.

Low-quantity samples also present challenges. In cases of "touch DNA," where genetic material is transferred through skin cells, the amount of DNA may be too small to yield a usable profile. Such limitations reduce the effectiveness of traditional DNA matching in solving crimes with minimal or compromised evidence.

2. Partial or Mixed DNA Profiles

Crime scenes often contain DNA from multiple individuals, leading to mixed profiles that are difficult to interpret. For example, in sexual assault cases, DNA from the victim, perpetrator, and potentially other contributors may be present. Traditional matching methods struggle to disentangle these complex mixtures, particularly when the contributors are closely related or when one contributor's DNA is present in much smaller amounts than the others.

Partial profiles, where only some genetic markers are detected, pose another challenge. While they can provide leads, they often lack the discriminatory power needed for a definitive identification. This limitation is especially problematic in cases where the suspect's DNA is not already in a database.

3. Reliance on Database Matches

Traditional DNA matching relies heavily on comparing a suspect's DNA to profiles stored in databases. If the perpetrator's profile is not already in a database, the investigation reaches a dead end. This limitation is particularly pronounced in cases involving first-time offenders or individuals who have managed to evade detection by law enforcement.

The effectiveness of database searches is contingent on the size and diversity of the database. Smaller databases with limited representation of certain populations reduce the likelihood of finding a match, perpetuating inequities in the justice system.

4. Inability to Identify Relatives

Traditional DNA matching focuses on exact matches, meaning it cannot identify relatives of a suspect. This limitation excludes a valuable avenue for generating investigative leads. For instance, if a perpetrator's DNA is not in a database, traditional methods cannot identify a close relative whose profile might provide a crucial link to the suspect.

5. False Matches and Statistical Limitations

While rare, false matches can occur in traditional DNA matching due to coincidental similarities in genetic markers. This risk is amplified in cases where statistical probabilities are misunderstood or misrepresented. For example, juries may be swayed by the "prosecutor's fallacy," in which the rarity of a DNA profile is conflated with the probability of a suspect's guilt.

6. Ethical and Legal Constraints

Traditional DNA matching raises ethical and legal concerns, particularly regarding privacy and consent. The collection of DNA from suspects, arrestees, or even innocent individuals has sparked debates about potential misuse and violations of civil liberties. Furthermore, disparities in how DNA evidence is collected and analyzed can lead to accusations of bias, particularly in communities that are over-policed.

7. Costs and Resource Limitations

In its early years, DNA testing was prohibitively expensive, limiting its use to high-profile cases. While costs have decreased over time, the expense of maintaining and expanding DNA databases, as well as processing backlogged samples, remains a significant barrier for many jurisdictions. Resource limitations also affect the speed and accuracy of analyses, with understaffed laboratories contributing to delays in investigations.

Addressing the Limitations

To overcome the challenges of traditional DNA matching, forensic science has embraced innovative approaches such as advanced sequencing technologies, probabilistic genotyping, and genetic genealogy. By broadening the scope of DNA analysis, these methods address many of the limitations discussed above.

For instance, genetic genealogy leverages the principles of familial DNA matching to identify relatives of unknown suspects, providing a powerful tool for generating leads in cases where traditional methods fall short. This approach, popularized by high-profile successes like the Golden State Killer case, has breathed new life into cold case investigations.

Emerging technologies such as next-generation sequencing (NGS) allow for the analysis of degraded or low-quantity samples, expanding the range of cases that can benefit from DNA evidence. Machine learning and artificial intelligence are also being integrated into forensic workflows, improving the interpretation of complex DNA mixtures and reducing the risk of human error.

The historical perspective on DNA evidence reveals a remarkable journey from its discovery to its transformative impact on criminal justice. While traditional DNA matching has revolutionized crime-solving, its limitations have highlighted the need for continuous innovation and adaptation. By understanding these constraints and investing in emerging technologies, law enforcement agencies and forensic scientists can further enhance their ability to solve crimes, bring justice to victims, and ensure the integrity of the judicial process.

III. The Birth of Genetic Genealogy in Law Enforcement

Genetic genealogy, the fusion of genetic science and genealogical research, has revolutionized law enforcement, enabling the resolution of cases that were previously considered unsolvable. The practice involves using DNA to uncover familial connections, creating a trail that can lead to the identification of suspects or victims in criminal investigations. While genetic genealogy has been a cornerstone of personal ancestry exploration for years, its introduction into law enforcement marked a significant turning point in forensic science.

Genesis of Genetic Genealogy

Genetic genealogy began as a tool for individuals seeking to uncover their ancestral roots. Companies like 23andMe, AncestryDNA, and MyHeritage popularized this technology in the early 2000s, allowing people to use DNA testing to trace their heritage and discover familial connections. By analyzing markers in the human genome, these services provided insights into ethnicity, ancestral migrations, and even potential relatives. The success and popularity of consumer DNA testing rapidly grew, leading to the development of extensive genetic databases that stored millions of DNA profiles.

While the use of these databases initially focused on personal and historical exploration, some pioneers recognized the potential for genetic genealogy to aid in criminal investigations. By leveraging DNA evidence left at crime scenes and cross-referencing it with profiles in these databases, investigators could identify familial connections to unknown individuals. This novel approach provided an unprecedented opportunity to crack cold cases where traditional DNA matching methods had failed.

Initial Forays into Criminal Investigations

The integration of genetic genealogy into law enforcement began in the mid-2010s. Unlike traditional DNA matching, which relies on finding exact matches in criminal databases such as CODIS (Combined DNA Index System), genetic genealogy uses partial matches to infer relationships with distant relatives. This method is particularly valuable in cases where a suspect's DNA profile is absent from law enforcement databases.

One of the earliest cases to benefit from genetic genealogy was the identification of Lisa Jensen, a woman who had been kidnapped as a child and whose true identity remained unknown for decades. In 2015, genealogist Barbara Rae-Venter employed genetic genealogy techniques to uncover Lisa's familial connections, eventually determining her biological identity. This success demonstrated the potential of genetic genealogy in solving complex cases, paving the way for its broader application in law enforcement.

Key Elements of Genetic Genealogy in Investigations

- DNA Analysis: Investigators analyze crime scene DNA using advanced testing methods to generate a genetic profile that can be uploaded to public databases.
- Database Search: The genetic profile is compared against profiles in public genealogy databases, such as GEDmatch and

FamilyTreeDNA, to identify potential familial matches.

- Family Tree Construction: Genealogists construct family trees based on the matches, using publicly available records such as birth certificates, marriage licenses, and obituaries.
- Suspect Identification: By narrowing down the family tree and cross-referencing it with other evidence, investigators identify a potential suspect.
- Verification: Law enforcement collects direct DNA evidence from the suspect, typically through discarded items, to confirm their identity.

These steps, while methodical and complex, provide a powerful framework for solving cold cases and identifying suspects who have evaded traditional investigative methods.

IV. The Golden State Killer Case: A Watershed Moment

The Golden State Killer case is the defining moment in the history of genetic genealogy in law enforcement. It not only showcased the immense potential of this technique but also cemented its role as a revolutionary tool in criminal investigations. The case, which had baffled investigators for decades, involved a series of heinous crimes committed by an elusive offender whose identity remained a mystery until the advent of genetic genealogy.

The Crimes of the Golden State Killer

The Golden State Killer, also known as the East Area Rapist and the Original Night Stalker, terrorized California during the 1970s and 1980s. Over a span of more than a decade, he was responsible for at least 13 murders, 51 rapes, and over 120 burglaries. His crimes were characterized by their brutality, meticulous planning, and the ability to evade capture despite leaving a trail of fear and devastation.

The perpetrator's modus operandi evolved over time. He began as a burglar in Visalia, breaking into homes and stealing valuables. Eventually, he escalated to sexual assaults, often targeting suburban neighborhoods and attacking women in their homes. His attacks were marked by calculated cruelty, as he would bind and blindfold his victims, sometimes forcing them to endure hours of psychological torment.

Later, he began killing his victims, leaving behind little evidence that could lead to his identification.

For decades, law enforcement agencies across California worked tirelessly to solve the case, but the Golden State Killer remained elusive. Traditional investigative methods, including eyewitness accounts, composite sketches, and the limited forensic tools available at the time, failed to produce viable leads. DNA evidence collected from crime scenes confirmed that the crimes were committed by the same individual, but without a match in criminal databases, investigators hit a dead end.

The Breakthrough: Genetic Genealogy

In 2018, a breakthrough came when investigators decided to employ genetic genealogy to solve the case. A crime scene DNA profile was uploaded to GEDmatch, a public genealogy database that allows users to compare their DNA with others to find relatives. This marked the first time genetic genealogy was used in a high-profile criminal investigation, and it quickly yielded results.

By analyzing partial matches in the database, genealogists identified distant relatives of the Golden State Killer. Using traditional genealogical research methods, they constructed family trees and traced the suspect's lineage. After narrowing down potential candidates, investigators focused on Joseph James DeAngelo, a former police officer who fit the profile of the elusive killer.

To confirm DeAngelo's identity, law enforcement collected a sample of his DNA from discarded items, such as a tissue. The DNA was analyzed and found to match the crime scene evidence, conclusively linking DeAngelo to the crimes. On April 24, 2018, he was arrested and charged with multiple counts of murder, finally bringing an end to the decades-long hunt for the Golden State Killer.

Impact on Law Enforcement

The resolution of the Golden State Killer case was a watershed moment for several reasons:

- Validation of Genetic Genealogy: The case demonstrated the effectiveness of genetic genealogy as a tool for solving cold cases, particularly those involving unidentified suspects who had evaded traditional methods.

- Renewed Interest in Cold Cases: Following the success of the Golden State Killer investigation, law enforcement agencies across the country began revisiting unsolved cases. Many of these cases, previously considered hopeless, were reopened with the hope of leveraging genetic genealogy to uncover new leads.

- Collaboration Between Genealogists and Law Enforcement: The case highlighted the importance of collaboration between professional genealogists and law enforcement agencies. Experts like Barbara Rae-Venter played a critical role in interpreting the genealogical data and identifying familial connections.

- Public Awareness and Ethical Debate: The case brought genetic genealogy into the public spotlight, sparking debates about privacy, consent, and the ethical implications of using consumer DNA databases for law enforcement purposes. While many celebrated the breakthrough, critics raised concerns about the potential misuse of genetic information and the need for clear legal guidelines.

Challenges and Controversies

While the success of the Golden State Killer case established genetic genealogy as a powerful investigative tool, it also raised important questions and challenges:

- Privacy Concerns: Critics argue that the use of public genealogy databases for criminal investigations raises privacy concerns. Many individuals who upload their DNA profiles to these databases do so for personal or genealogical purposes, not anticipating that their data could be used to identify relatives involved in criminal activities.

- Legal and Ethical Issues: The lack of a clear legal framework governing the use of genetic genealogy in law enforcement has sparked debates about consent, data ownership, and the potential for misuse. Some argue that law enforcement should obtain warrants before accessing genetic databases, while others advocate for stricter regulations to protect users' rights.

- Resource Intensive: Genetic genealogy investigations require significant time, expertise, and resources. Building family trees, verifying relationships, and cross-referencing records are labor-intensive tasks that may strain law enforcement budgets and personnel.

- Risk of Misidentification: While genetic genealogy is highly effective, there is always a risk of misidentification or false leads, particularly in cases involving complex family dynamics or endogamy (marriage within a small, closely related group).

The Legacy of the Golden State Killer Case

The Golden State Killer case remains a landmark in the history of criminal investigations, illustrating the transformative potential of genetic genealogy. It not only solved one of the most notorious crime sprees in U.S. history but also opened new avenues for justice in cases that had long been considered unsolvable.

Since the resolution of the Golden State Killer case, genetic genealogy has been used to solve numerous cold cases, bringing closure to victims' families and holding perpetrators accountable. Its success has inspired continued innovation in forensic science, including the development of advanced DNA testing techniques and expanded databases.

The case also serves as a reminder of the delicate balance between technological innovation and ethical responsibility. As genetic genealogy continues to shape the future of law enforcement, society must grapple with the implications of this powerful tool, ensuring that its benefits are realized while safeguarding individual rights and privacy.

Chapter 2: Understanding Genetic Genealogy

I.   Basic Principles of DNA Inheritance

Deoxyribonucleic acid, or DNA, is the molecular blueprint for all living organisms. It carries genetic instructions necessary for growth, development, and reproduction. DNA is composed of a double helix structure, with each strand consisting of sequences of nucleotides. These nucleotides include four bases: adenine (A), thymine (T), cytosine (C), and guanine (G). The sequence of these bases determines genetic traits, and the way DNA is passed down through generations forms the basis for genetic inheritance.

DNA and Chromosomes

Human DNA is organized into 23 pairs of chromosomes, totaling 46 in all. Each pair consists of one chromosome from the mother and one from the father. Among these are 22 pairs of autosomes and one pair of sex chromosomes, which determine biological sex. Females inherit two X chromosomes (one from each parent), while males inherit one X chromosome from their mother and one Y chromosome from their father. This chromosomal structure underpins the inheritance patterns observed in families.

Patterns of Inheritance

DNA is inherited in predictable ways; which genetic genealogists use to trace relationships:

- Autosomal DNA: This is found in the 22 pairs of autosomes and is inherited equally from both parents. Half of a person's autosomal DNA comes from their mother, and half from their father. Because this DNA recombines with each generation, distant relationships are harder to detect.
- Y-DNA: The Y chromosome is passed directly from father to son with little change, making it a reliable marker for tracing paternal ancestry. It is useful for studying surname patterns and male lineage.
- Mitochondrial DNA (mtDNA): Found outside the cell nucleus in mitochondria, mtDNA is passed from mothers to all their children. It remains relatively unchanged across generations, making it a valuable tool for studying maternal ancestry.

Recombination and Mutations

One of the key processes in genetic inheritance is recombination, which occurs during the formation of reproductive cells (sperm and eggs). Recombination mixes genetic material from the parents, creating unique DNA profiles for each offspring. Additionally, mutations—small changes in the DNA sequence—can occur. These mutations can serve as markers for identifying genetic relationships and tracing ancestry over long periods.

II.   Types of DNA Testing

Genetic genealogy leverages three main types of DNA testing to investigate relationships and build family trees: Y-DNA, mtDNA, and autosomal DNA testing. Each type offers unique insights into genetic heritage and is suited for specific purposes in genealogical research.

1. Y-DNA Testing

Overview:

Y-DNA testing examines the Y chromosome, which is unique to males and passed directly from father to son. This type of testing focuses on the non-recombining portions of the Y chromosome, which remain relatively unchanged across generations.

Applications:

- Tracing Paternal Lineage: Since the Y chromosome is only present in males, it provides a clear picture of the direct paternal line, or "surname line."

- Surname Studies: Y-DNA testing can confirm whether two males with the same surname share a common ancestor.
- Population Studies: It helps identify haplogroups—genetic populations that share a common ancestor—providing insights into deep ancestral origins.

Markers Analyzed:

Y-DNA tests analyze specific markers known as short tandem repeats (STRs) and single nucleotide polymorphisms (SNPs). STRs are repetitive sequences of DNA that can vary in length, while SNPs are single base changes in the DNA sequence. STRs are useful for identifying recent relationships, while SNPs reveal deeper ancestral connections.

Limitations:

- Only males can take Y-DNA tests, though females can explore their paternal lineage by testing a close male relative.

- The Y chromosome provides information only about the direct paternal line and does not account for other branches of ancestry.

2. Mitochondrial DNA (mtDNA) Testing

Overview:

Unlike Y-DNA, mtDNA is passed down from mothers to all their children, regardless of sex. This makes mtDNA testing a powerful tool for tracing maternal ancestry.

Applications:

- Maternal Lineage: mtDNA testing can trace a person's maternal line back thousands of years.
- Deep Ancestry: mtDNA haplogroups provide insights into ancient migration patterns and ethnic origins.
- Identifying Relationships: It can confirm maternal connections between individuals, particularly in cases where traditional genealogical records are missing.

Markers Analyzed:

mtDNA tests analyze the hypervariable regions (HVR1 and HVR2) and the coding region of the mitochondrial genome. These regions are prone to mutations, which serve as markers for tracing ancestry.

Limitations:

- mtDNA is inherited as a single unit and does not recombine, so it provides no information about other lines of ancestry.
- Maternal ancestry can be challenging to interpret due to the limited variation in mtDNA over time.

3. Autosomal DNA Testing

Overview:

Autosomal DNA testing examines the 22 pairs of autosomes inherited from both parents. This type of test is the most comprehensive for genealogical purposes because it analyzes DNA from all ancestral lines.

Applications:

- Relationship Matching: Autosomal DNA tests are widely used to identify relatives within five to seven generations. They estimate the degree of relatedness based on shared segments of DNA.
- Ethnicity Estimates: These tests provide percentages of ancestry from different regions, offering insights into ethnic heritage.
- Building Family Trees: Autosomal DNA results can help construct detailed family trees by identifying genetic matches.

Markers Analyzed:

Autosomal DNA tests analyze thousands of single nucleotide polymorphisms (SNPs) spread across the genome. These markers provide the basis for comparing genetic material between individuals.

Limitations:

- The effectiveness of autosomal testing diminishes with distance; it may not reliably detect relationships beyond fourth or fifth cousins.

- Ethnicity estimates can vary between testing companies due to differences in reference populations and algorithms.

Comparison of DNA Testing Types

Type	Inheritance Pattern	Purpose	Strengths	Limitations
Y-DNA	Paternal (father to son)	Tracing paternal lineage	Clear paternal line; haplogroup identification	Male-only; limited to direct paternal line
mtDNA	Maternal (mother to children)	Tracing maternal lineage	Deep maternal ancestry; long-term stability	No information on other lines; less variation

Type	Inheritance Pattern	Purpose	Strengths	Limitations
				in results
Autosomal DNA	Inherited from both parents	Comprehensive genealogical research	Identifies relationships across all lines; ethnicity estimates	Limited to 5–7 generations; ethnicity results may vary

Choosing the Right Test

The choice of DNA test depends on the goals of the research:

- For exploring paternal lineage, a Y-DNA test is ideal, particularly for surname studies.
- To investigate maternal ancestry, mtDNA testing offers the most direct results.

- Autosomal DNA testing is best for building family trees, finding close relatives, and exploring ethnic heritage.

DNA Testing in Practice

The application of these DNA testing methods has revolutionized genealogy and criminal investigations. For example:

- Cold Case Solving: Y-DNA and autosomal DNA testing have been instrumental in solving decades-old cold cases by identifying perpetrators through family members.
- Adoption Research: Autosomal DNA testing is commonly used by adoptees to find biological relatives.
- Ancestry Research: Millions of people use DNA testing to uncover their ethnic roots and connect with distant relatives.

Ethical and Privacy Considerations

The rise of DNA testing has brought privacy concerns to the forefront. Many commercial databases allow users to opt out of law enforcement access, while others actively collaborate with agencies. The ethical use of DNA data remains a topic of debate, particularly regarding consent and the implications of uncovering unexpected family relationships.

The principles of DNA inheritance and the various types of DNA testing offer powerful tools for understanding our genetic makeup, tracing ancestry, and solving mysteries. Whether used for genealogical research or criminal investigations, these technologies have transformed the way we connect with the past and present. By understanding the unique capabilities and limitations of Y-DNA, mtDNA, and autosomal DNA testing, researchers can make informed decisions to achieve their goals while navigating the ethical and practical challenges of genetic analysis.

III. How Genetic Relationships Are Measured

Genetic relationships are measured by analyzing the amount and arrangement of shared DNA between individuals. DNA is passed from parents to their children in predictable ways, allowing scientists and genealogists to determine familial connections with remarkable accuracy. The measurement of these relationships relies on concepts such as shared segments, centimorgans (cM), and the degree of recombination.

Shared Segments

DNA is organized into chromosomes, with specific regions inherited from each parent. When individuals share common ancestors, they inherit identical segments of DNA from those ancestors. These shared segments of DNA are the primary indicators of genetic relationships.

- Length of Segments: Longer shared segments indicate closer relationships, as there has been less opportunity for recombination to break down the inherited DNA over generations.
- Number of Segments: The total number of shared DNA segments also provides clues about the degree of relatedness.

Centimorgans (cM)

Centimorgans (cM) are a unit of measurement used to quantify the amount of shared DNA between two individuals. One centimorgan represents a probability of 1% that a segment of DNA will be recombined during meiosis.

- Close Relatives: Close relatives, such as siblings or parents, typically share hundreds or even thousands of centimorgans. For instance, full siblings share approximately 2,600–3,400 cM.

- Distant Relatives: More distant relatives, such as third or fourth cousins, share much smaller amounts of DNA, often in the range of 20–100 cM.

- Thresholds: Most genetic testing companies set thresholds for shared DNA to exclude distant or spurious matches, ensuring more accurate predictions of familial relationships.

Relationship Predictions

Using shared segments and centimorgan data, algorithms can predict the likely relationship between two individuals. These predictions take into account both the total shared DNA and the distribution of shared segments across chromosomes. However, some ambiguity exists, as certain relationships (e.g., half-siblings vs. aunts/uncles) may produce similar patterns of shared DNA.

Tools for Measuring Relationships

- Segment Mapping: Tools like chromosome browsers allow users to visualize shared segments, helping identify the specific regions of DNA inherited from a common ancestor.
- Cluster Analysis: Genetic clustering techniques group matches based on shared DNA, revealing connections between extended family members.
- Triangulation: By comparing shared segments among three or more individuals, genealogists can confirm shared ancestry and pinpoint the common ancestor.

IV. Commercial DNA Databases and Their Role

Commercial DNA databases have revolutionized genetic genealogy and cold case investigations by providing access to vast repositories of genetic data. These databases connect millions of users, enabling the identification of relatives, the construction of family trees, and the resolution of long-standing mysteries.

Key Players in the Industry

Several major companies dominate the field of consumer DNA testing, each offering unique features and services:

AncestryDNA:

- The largest consumer DNA database, with over 20 million users.
- Focuses on ethnicity estimates and family tree integration.
- Provides powerful tools for identifying genetic matches.

23andMe:

- Offers health-related genetic reports alongside ancestry information.
- Emphasizes scientific analysis of genetic traits and conditions.
- Known for its user-friendly interface and large database.

MyHeritage DNA:

- Popular for its global reach and support for diverse populations.
- Specializes in ethnicity estimates and historical record integration.

FamilyTreeDNA (FTDNA):

- The only major company offering Y-DNA and mtDNA tests alongside autosomal testing.
- Frequently used by serious genealogists and researchers.

GEDmatch:

- A free platform that allows users to upload raw DNA data from other companies.
- Known for its role in law enforcement investigations.

Uses in Genealogy

Commercial DNA databases serve a variety of purposes for genealogists:

- Finding Relatives: By comparing DNA profiles, users can identify close and distant relatives within the database.

- Building Family Trees: Shared DNA matches provide clues for reconstructing family histories.
- Ethnicity Estimates: Databases use reference populations to estimate a user's ethnic origins, offering insights into ancestral migration patterns.

Law Enforcement Applications

Commercial DNA databases have become indispensable tools for solving cold cases and identifying unknown individuals. Genetic genealogy combines traditional family tree research with DNA evidence to identify suspects or victims.

- Famous Cases: The arrest of the Golden State Killer in 2018 demonstrated the power of these databases in criminal investigations. Law enforcement used GEDmatch to identify the perpetrator through distant relatives.
- Techniques: Investigators upload DNA profiles from crime scenes to public databases, then use genetic matches to trace family trees back to the individual of interest.

V.   Privacy Considerations

The widespread use of commercial DNA databases has raised significant privacy concerns. These platforms store sensitive genetic information that could potentially be misused or accessed without consent.

Key Concerns

Unauthorized Access:

- Genetic data stored in databases may be vulnerable to hacking or unauthorized access.
- Users may inadvertently expose relatives' genetic information by uploading their own DNA.

Law Enforcement Use:

- The use of genetic databases by law enforcement has sparked debates about privacy and consent.
- Critics argue that individuals should not be subject to genetic searches without explicit approval.

Third-Party Sharing:

- Some companies share anonymized genetic data with third parties, including pharmaceutical and research organizations.
- While this data is often used for medical advancements, it raises ethical questions about informed consent.

Familial Implications:

- DNA testing can reveal unexpected relationships, such as previously unknown siblings or non-paternity events, potentially causing emotional distress.

Consent Policies

Most DNA testing companies require users to provide explicit consent for certain uses of their data, including participation in law enforcement investigations or research studies.

- Opt-In/Opt-Out Options: Companies like GEDmatch offer users the ability to opt in or out of law enforcement matching.
- Transparency: Reputable companies publish detailed privacy policies outlining how genetic data is used, shared, and protected.

VI.   Legal Framework

The legal framework governing DNA databases varies widely by country and is often lagging behind technological advancements. Key areas of concern include data ownership, consent, and the ethical use of genetic information.

United States

Federal Laws:

- The Genetic Information Nondiscrimination Act (GINA) prohibits the use of genetic information in employment and health insurance decisions.
- The Health Insurance Portability and Accountability Act (HIPAA) protects medical records, including genetic information, within the healthcare system.

State Laws:

- Some states have enacted laws limiting law enforcement access to commercial DNA databases.
- Regulations differ significantly between states, creating a patchwork of legal protections.

Law Enforcement Access:

- Courts have upheld the use of public DNA databases by law enforcement, as users voluntarily upload their genetic data.
- Private databases like AncestryDNA and 23andMe have policies against law enforcement use without a warrant.

European Union

General Data Protection Regulation (GDPR):

- The GDPR establishes stringent rules for the collection, storage, and use of genetic data.
- Individuals have the right to access, correct, and delete their genetic data stored by companies.

Ethical Guidelines:

- European countries emphasize the ethical implications of genetic testing, particularly in criminal investigations.

- Law enforcement access is generally more restricted than in the U.S.

Other Countries

- Canada: Genetic data is protected under privacy laws, but there is limited regulation specific to consumer DNA testing.
- Australia: Privacy legislation governs the use of genetic information, with an emphasis on protecting individuals from discrimination.
- Developing Nations: Many countries lack comprehensive legal frameworks for genetic data, leaving consumers vulnerable to potential misuse.

Balancing Innovation and Privacy

As DNA testing technology continues to advance, striking a balance between innovation and privacy will be critical. Policymakers, companies, and researchers must collaborate to establish ethical standards and legal protections that safeguard individual rights while enabling the transformative potential of genetic data.

- Transparency: Clear communication about data usage and consent is essential for building trust with consumers.
- Legislation: Governments must update laws to address emerging privacy concerns and regulate law enforcement access.
- Education: Public awareness campaigns can help individuals make informed decisions about participating in DNA testing and database sharing.

The measurement of genetic relationships, the role of commercial DNA databases, and the complexities of privacy considerations form the foundation of modern genetic genealogy. While these technologies offer unparalleled opportunities for discovery, they also raise significant ethical and legal challenges. By understanding how genetic relationships are measured, the role of DNA databases, and the frameworks that protect privacy, individuals and organizations can navigate this rapidly evolving field responsibly and effectively.

Part II: The Investigation Process

Chapter 3: Building the Genetic Profile

I. Collection and Preservation of DNA Evidence

The Importance of DNA Evidence in Criminal Investigations

DNA evidence has revolutionized criminal investigations, offering a level of precision that other forensic methods cannot match. Its ability to uniquely identify individuals based on their genetic makeup has made it an invaluable tool for solving crimes, both recent and decades-old. However, the reliability of DNA evidence depends heavily on its collection and preservation. Improper handling can compromise its integrity, leading to inconclusive results or even wrongful convictions.

Collecting DNA Evidence

Effective DNA collection requires meticulous techniques to avoid contamination and ensure that the evidence is suitable for analysis. Common sources of DNA include blood, saliva, hair, skin cells, sweat, semen, and other bodily fluids. These materials can be found on a variety of surfaces, such as clothing, weapons, furniture, and even in the environment.

- Identifying Potential DNA Sources: The first step in DNA collection is identifying the locations where DNA is most likely to be found. Crime scene investigators (CSIs) examine the crime scene meticulously, looking for signs of struggle, blood spatter, or objects that the perpetrator may have touched. For instance, a discarded cigarette butt, a used drinking glass, or a hair follicle could all provide viable DNA samples.

- Collection Methods: Once potential DNA sources are identified, specialized tools and techniques are used to collect samples:

- Swabbing: This is the most common method for collecting DNA. Sterile cotton swabs or foam-tipped applicators are moistened with distilled water and used to swab surfaces suspected of harboring DNA. Swabs are then air-dried before being stored in sterile containers.

- Cutting or Scraping: For dried biological material, such as blood on fabric or skin cells on a weapon, CSIs may cut out sections of the material or scrape it to collect evidence.

- Vacuum Collection: When DNA is suspected to be present in a large area or on a porous surface, a specialized vacuum device equipped with a filter can be used to collect trace evidence.

- Minimizing Contamination Risks: Contamination is a major concern during DNA collection. Investigators follow strict protocols to prevent the introduction of foreign DNA:

- Wearing gloves, masks, and disposable clothing to avoid shedding their own DNA.

- Using sterilized tools and materials for each sample.

- Ensuring that DNA samples are collected and stored in separate containers to prevent cross-contamination.

Preserving DNA Evidence

The preservation of DNA evidence is as critical as its collection. DNA degrades over time due to environmental factors like heat, moisture, and exposure to chemicals or UV light. Proper preservation ensures that samples remain viable for analysis, even after decades.

Storage Conditions

- Temperature Control: DNA samples must be kept at cool or freezing temperatures to slow degradation. Biological materials like blood or saliva are often refrigerated, while extracted DNA is stored in freezers at -20°C or lower.

- Humidity Management: Excessive moisture promotes the growth of bacteria and fungi, which can destroy DNA. Evidence should be stored in a dry environment, and samples must be completely dry before packaging.

Packaging and Labeling

- DNA evidence is typically stored in paper bags or envelopes rather than plastic, as plastic can trap moisture and encourage microbial growth.

- Each item is carefully labeled with details such as the case number, collection date, location, and description. This documentation ensures proper chain-of-custody management, which is crucial for legal admissibility.

- Long-Term Storage: For cases that remain unsolved for years or decades, long-term preservation methods are employed. DNA samples are periodically checked to ensure their integrity, and advancements in preservation technology, such as the use of desiccants or vacuum-sealed storage, are utilized to enhance longevity.

Challenges in DNA Collection and Preservation

Despite advances in forensic science, several challenges persist:

- Environmental Contamination: DNA samples found outdoors are often exposed to sunlight, rain, and other environmental factors that degrade DNA.
- Trace Evidence: Small or degraded samples may not contain enough DNA for analysis. Techniques like polymerase chain reaction (PCR) are used to amplify these samples, but the initial collection must still be meticulous.
- Old Evidence: Many cold cases involve evidence collected decades ago, before modern DNA preservation techniques were

established. The quality of such evidence can vary significantly.

II. Converting Old Samples to Modern DNA Profiles

The Importance of Updating DNA Profiles

Advancements in DNA analysis technology have made it possible to revisit old cases with greater precision. Converting old DNA samples to modern profiles allows investigators to apply new techniques, search current databases, and potentially identify individuals who were previously untraceable.

Challenges with Old DNA Samples

Old DNA samples often present unique difficulties:

- Degradation: Over time, DNA breaks down into smaller fragments, making it harder to analyze. Factors like improper storage, environmental exposure, and the age of the sample exacerbate degradation.
- Contamination: Evidence collected before the implementation of strict protocols may contain contaminating DNA from investigators, medical personnel, or others who handled the evidence.

- Technological Limitations of the Past: Older DNA analyses relied on techniques like restriction fragment length polymorphism (RFLP), which required large quantities of high-quality DNA. These methods are less sensitive and less discriminatory compared to modern approaches.

Modern DNA Analysis Techniques

To convert old samples into usable modern DNA profiles, forensic scientists employ a variety of advanced techniques:

DNA Extraction and Purification

- Scientists extract DNA from the biological material using methods tailored to the type of sample (e.g., blood, bone, hair).
- Advanced purification techniques remove contaminants, such as proteins and chemicals, that may interfere with analysis.

Polymerase Chain Reaction (PCR)

PCR is a revolutionary technique that amplifies small amounts of DNA into quantities sufficient for analysis.

Even trace or degraded samples can be analyzed using PCR, as long as some intact DNA remains.

- Mini-STR Analysis: For highly degraded DNA, short tandem repeat (STR) analysis focuses on shorter DNA segments, which are more likely to remain intact over time. Mini-STRs are particularly useful in cold cases.

- Mitochondrial DNA (mtDNA) Analysis: Mitochondrial DNA is more abundant and resilient than nuclear DNA, making it useful for analyzing degraded or minimal samples. MtDNA is especially valuable for identifying remains or familial relationships when nuclear DNA is insufficient.

- Next-Generation Sequencing (NGS): NGS represents the cutting edge of DNA analysis. This technology sequences entire genomes, providing more detailed and comprehensive genetic profiles. It is particularly effective for mixed or degraded samples, as it can analyze complex DNA mixtures.

Y-STR and X-STR Analysis

- Y-STR analysis focuses on the Y chromosome, which is passed down through the male lineage. This technique is useful for identifying male contributors in cases involving mixed samples.
- X-STR analysis, though less commonly used, can help trace genetic relationships in complex familial structures.

Overcoming Old Sample Challenges

Forensic laboratories employ innovative methods to overcome the unique challenges posed by old DNA samples:

- Bone and Teeth Analysis: In cases where soft tissues have deteriorated, bones and teeth serve as robust DNA sources. Advanced techniques allow for the extraction of DNA from these materials, even after decades.
- Contaminant Removal: Modern protocols include steps to identify and remove contaminating DNA. Bioinformatics tools can differentiate between human DNA and contaminants, ensuring the accuracy of the genetic profile.

Case Studies in Old Sample Conversion

- The Golden State Killer Case: DNA from decades-old crime scenes was successfully analyzed using modern genetic genealogy techniques, leading to the identification and conviction of Joseph James DeAngelo.

- World War II Remains: Advances in mtDNA analysis have enabled the identification of soldiers' remains from World War II, bringing closure to families after nearly 80 years.

The Role of Genetic Genealogy

Once old samples are converted into modern DNA profiles, genetic genealogy plays a crucial role in solving cases. By comparing these profiles to those in commercial DNA databases, investigators can identify familial connections that lead to suspects or unidentified victims.

Ethical and Legal Considerations

The conversion of old DNA samples raises ethical and legal questions:

- Consent: Should investigators use DNA collected decades ago for purposes not originally intended, such as genetic genealogy?
- Privacy: How can agencies balance the need for justice with individuals' privacy rights?
- Legal Admissibility: Courts must decide whether DNA evidence converted from old samples meets current standards for admissibility.

The collection and preservation of DNA evidence, along with the conversion of old samples to modern DNA profiles, are cornerstones of forensic science. These processes enable investigators to revisit cold cases, using state-of-the-art technology to uncover the truth. While challenges persist, ongoing advancements in DNA analysis and preservation hold the promise of solving cases that once seemed unsolvable. By adhering to rigorous standards and addressing ethical concerns, the potential for justice through DNA evidence continues to expand, offering hope to victims and their families.

III.   Choosing   the   Right   DNA   Testing
        Company

**The Role of DNA Testing Companies in Criminal
Investigations**

DNA testing companies are central to modern investigative efforts, especially in cases involving genetic genealogy. These companies provide the technical expertise, laboratory infrastructure, and access to genetic databases necessary to analyze DNA evidence effectively. Choosing the right DNA testing company can significantly impact the success of an investigation, particularly in cold cases where older or degraded DNA samples require specialized handling.

**Key Considerations for Choosing a DNA Testing
Company**

- Testing Capabilities: Not all DNA testing companies offer the same services. It is essential to select a company equipped to handle the specific needs of the investigation.
- Comprehensive DNA Analysis: Look for companies that offer a range of testing options, including autosomal DNA, Y-DNA, and

mitochondrial DNA analysis. These methods provide a broader spectrum of genetic information, increasing the likelihood of a successful match.

- Advanced Technologies: Companies utilizing cutting-edge techniques such as next-generation sequencing (NGS) are better suited for analyzing degraded or complex DNA samples.

- Custom Solutions for Old Samples: In cold case investigations, companies with expertise in handling degraded or trace DNA samples are invaluable.

Database Access

- The size and accessibility of a company's database significantly influence the likelihood of identifying genetic connections.

- Public vs. Private Databases: Companies that allow law enforcement access to their databases, such as GEDmatch and FamilyTreeDNA, are preferred for criminal investigations.

- Database Size: Larger databases increase the probability of finding matches, as they contain more genetic profiles.

Compliance with Legal and Ethical Standards

- Privacy Policies: The company must adhere to legal standards governing data privacy, including clear policies for obtaining user consent for law enforcement access.
- Transparency: Companies should be transparent about how they handle, store, and share genetic data.
- Accreditation: Look for companies accredited by organizations such as the American Association for Laboratory Accreditation (A2LA) or the International Organization for Standardization (ISO).

Reputation and Track Record

A company's history of success in supporting criminal investigations is an important factor.

- Investigators should consider companies with proven results in solving cold cases or other high-profile cases.

- Reviews, case studies, and endorsements from law enforcement agencies provide valuable insights into a company's capabilities.

Turnaround Time and Cost

- Efficiency: While some investigations may not have urgent deadlines, a company's ability to deliver results quickly can be critical in active cases.
- Budget Considerations: High-quality testing often comes at a higher cost, but agencies must balance this with the potential benefits of obtaining accurate and actionable results.

IV. Upload Procedures to Genealogical Databases

Why Genealogical Databases Are Crucial

Genealogical databases have transformed the landscape of criminal investigations by enabling connections between DNA profiles and potential relatives of suspects or victims. These databases contain genetic information voluntarily submitted by individuals, often for ancestry or health insights. By uploading DNA profiles to these platforms, investigators can use shared genetic markers to identify familial relationships, providing crucial leads in cases that might otherwise remain unsolved.

The Process of Uploading DNA Profiles

Uploading DNA profiles to genealogical databases involves several steps, each requiring precision and adherence to legal guidelines.

Preparing the DNA Profile

- Conversion to Compatible Format: Before uploading, the DNA profile generated by forensic analysis must be converted into a format compatible with the database. Most genealogical databases use raw DNA data in standard file formats like .txt or .csv, containing information on genetic markers and their corresponding alleles.
- Ensuring Data Integrity: The DNA profile must be thoroughly reviewed for accuracy, as errors in the data could lead to false matches or missed connections.

Choosing the Database

- GEDmatch: One of the most widely used databases for law enforcement, GEDmatch allows users to upload DNA profiles from various testing companies. It includes tools specifically designed for genetic genealogy, such as relationship estimators and segment mapping.
- FamilyTreeDNA: Another platform that permits law enforcement access, FamilyTreeDNA has a large user base and offers comprehensive matching tools.
- AncestryDNA and 23andMe: While these companies have larger databases, they currently restrict law enforcement access without explicit user consent.

Creating a User Profile

Investigators must create a user profile within the database, ensuring transparency and compliance with the platform's terms of service.

- The profile should clearly indicate that it is being used for investigative purposes.

- Most databases require law enforcement to specify whether the DNA belongs to a victim, suspect, or unknown individual.

Uploading the DNA Data

- The raw DNA data is uploaded to the database via a secure interface.
- Investigators must provide metadata about the sample, such as the date it was collected and its relevance to the case.

Opting Into Law Enforcement Matching

- Many databases offer users the option to allow or restrict matches for law enforcement purposes. Investigators must ensure that the uploaded profile is flagged for law enforcement matching, if permitted.

Challenges in Upload Procedures

- Data Compatibility: Not all DNA profiles are immediately compatible with genealogical databases, requiring conversion or additional analysis.

- Privacy Concerns: Users' consent is a critical factor, and investigators must navigate varying policies across platforms.
- Incomplete Matches: Matches found in databases often represent distant relatives, requiring extensive genealogical research to establish connections.

V. Quality Control and Verification

Why Quality Control Matters

Ensuring the accuracy and reliability of DNA evidence is paramount in criminal investigations. Quality control and verification processes are designed to minimize errors, prevent contamination, and ensure that conclusions drawn from DNA evidence are scientifically sound.

Quality Control in DNA Testing

Laboratory Standards

- DNA testing laboratories must follow strict quality control protocols, including accreditation by recognized organizations like ISO or the FBI's Quality Assurance Standards (QAS).

- Regular audits and proficiency testing are conducted to maintain high standards of accuracy and reliability.

Validation of Methods

- Laboratories must validate all testing methods and instruments before use.
- Validation involves testing the method's sensitivity, specificity, and reproducibility across different sample types and conditions.

Replication of Results

- Critical DNA samples are often tested multiple times to confirm results.
- Replication ensures that findings are consistent and not the result of procedural errors or contamination.

Verification of Genealogical Matches

Confirming Relationships

- Once a match is identified in a genealogical database, additional analysis is conducted to verify the relationship. This may involve examining shared DNA segments, testing additional family members, or cross-referencing with documentary evidence like birth and marriage records.

- Tools like chromosome browsers and segment mapping software are used to analyze genetic data at a granular level.

Avoiding False Positives

- False positives can occur due to coincidental genetic similarities, endogamy, or incomplete datasets. Investigators must corroborate genetic matches with other evidence to avoid misidentifications.

- Advanced statistical models are used to assess the likelihood of a true match.

Chain of Custody and Documentation

Maintaining a clear chain of custody for DNA evidence and all subsequent analyses is critical:

- Every step of the testing and upload process must be documented, including who handled the evidence, where it was stored, and how it was processed.

- Detailed documentation ensures that the evidence is admissible in court and that its integrity is beyond question.

Case Studies in Quality Control and Verification

The Golden State Killer Investigation

- Rigorous quality control measures ensured the accuracy of the DNA profile uploaded to genealogical databases, leading to the successful identification and conviction of Joseph James DeAngelo.

The 1974 Carla Walker Case

- Advanced verification processes confirmed a DNA match, solving a decades-old cold case and leading to the conviction of the perpetrator.

Overcoming Challenges in Quality Control

- Limited Resources: Smaller agencies may lack access to high-quality laboratories or genealogical expertise, requiring collaboration with larger organizations or private firms.
- Evolving Standards: As technology advances, laboratories must continuously update their

protocols to stay at the forefront of forensic science.

- Human Error: Extensive training and automation of processes can reduce the risk of human error during DNA testing and data analysis.

Choosing the right DNA testing company, executing proper upload procedures to genealogical databases, and implementing robust quality control and verification measures are critical components of using genetic genealogy in criminal investigations. These steps ensure that DNA evidence is handled with scientific rigor, enabling investigators to solve cold cases with confidence and integrity. By adhering to these best practices, law enforcement agencies can unlock the full potential of genetic genealogy to bring justice to victims and their families.

Chapter 4: Genealogical Research Methods

Genetic genealogy has revolutionized cold case investigations, bringing a new dimension to law enforcement by leveraging the power of DNA and genealogical research. Central to the success of this approach are two core processes: creating family trees and applying triangulation techniques. These tools help connect genetic data to specific individuals and their family networks, facilitating breakthroughs in long-unsolved cases. This chapter explores the intricacies of these methods, emphasizing their roles in solving the "unsolvable."

I. Creating Family Trees: Mapping Genetic Relationships

Creating a family tree is one of the fundamental steps in genetic genealogy. It involves systematically mapping relationships based on genetic matches identified through DNA databases and traditional genealogical records. This step bridges the gap between raw genetic data and the identities of individuals within a suspect's or victim's familial network.

Understanding Genetic Matches

When a DNA profile is uploaded to a genealogical database, it identifies individuals who share portions of their DNA with the subject. These genetic matches, categorized by the amount of shared DNA (measured in centimorgans or cM), provide critical clues about how individuals might be related. Matches with higher shared DNA amounts, such as 50% (e.g., parent-child relationships), are closer relatives, while matches with lower amounts suggest distant cousins.

The Initial Stages: Starting the Family Tree

The process begins with the closest genetic matches. For example, a match sharing 800 cM might be a first cousin. Genealogists use information provided by the database, such as family surnames, locations, or family trees created by other users, to identify common ancestors.

From here, genealogists systematically work backward through generations, incorporating additional genetic matches and public records like birth, marriage, and death certificates. This approach helps establish a comprehensive framework of the subject's ancestry.

Key Records and Resources

Genealogists rely heavily on traditional records, including:

- Census Records: These provide names, ages, family relationships, and places of residence.
- Vital Records: Birth, marriage, and death certificates validate familial connections and timelines.
- Historical Documents: Land records, military drafts, and wills can help trace lineage.
- Online Databases: Platforms like Ancestry.com and FamilySearch offer digitized family trees and archival data.

Combining DNA data with these resources enables investigators to corroborate genetic connections with documented familial ties.

Challenges in Family Tree Construction

Despite its importance, creating family trees is not without obstacles:

- Incomplete or Missing Records: Historical gaps due to war, migration, or poor record-keeping complicate lineage tracking.

- Adoptions and Non-Paternity Events (NPEs): These events, where the biological parent differs from the presumed parent, can disrupt traditional genealogical assumptions.
- Endogamy: Communities with high rates of intermarriage (e.g., Ashkenazi Jews or certain Appalachian groups) produce inflated genetic matches, complicating tree construction.

Overcoming these challenges often requires advanced problem-solving, creative approaches, and collaboration with historians or local experts.

II. Triangulation Techniques: Confirming Relationships

While creating family trees provides a foundational map, triangulation techniques validate and refine these relationships. Triangulation involves comparing DNA segments shared between the subject and multiple matches to identify common ancestors.

What Is Triangulation?

In genetic genealogy, triangulation is the process of identifying shared DNA segments across three or more individuals who are known or suspected relatives. The goal is to determine whether these shared segments originate from the same ancestor.

- Shared Segments: DNA databases like GEDmatch and MyHeritage provide tools to view shared DNA segments between individuals. For example, if three matches all share a specific segment on chromosome 7, it's likely they inherited this segment from a common ancestor.
- Cluster Analysis: Matches are grouped into clusters based on shared DNA segments. These clusters often represent distinct family lines, helping genealogists focus their research on specific branches of the family tree.

The Triangulation Process

Step 1: Identifying Shared DNA Segments

The first step in triangulation is identifying genetic matches who share DNA segments with the subject. Advanced DNA analysis tools visualize these segments, often in the form of chromosome browsers.

Step 2: Comparing Matches

Matches sharing overlapping DNA segments are compared to determine their likely relationship. For example:

- A subject shares 60 cM with Person A and 75 cM with Person B.
- Both matches share the same segment on Chromosome 3 with the subject.

This overlap suggests that Person A and Person B are related to each other through the same ancestral line.

Step 3: Tracing the Common Ancestor

Genealogists then integrate traditional genealogical records to trace the common ancestor responsible for the shared DNA. For example, if Person A and Person B both descend from John Doe (b. 1800), the subject is likely also related to John Doe.

Practical Applications of Triangulation

Triangulation plays a critical role in refining family trees and confirming connections. For instance:

- Narrowing Suspect Pools: If multiple distant cousins are identified, triangulation can pinpoint the specific ancestral branch leading to the subject.
- Confirming Relationships: Triangulation validates assumptions made during family tree construction, ensuring accuracy.
- Identifying False Matches: Some genetic matches occur by chance, particularly for very small shared DNA segments. Triangulation helps filter out these false positives.

Integrating Family Trees and Triangulation in Cold Case Investigations

Creating family trees and applying triangulation techniques often work in tandem during cold case investigations. Together, these processes narrow down suspect pools and identify connections between individuals and crime scenes.

Case Study: The Golden State Killer

The Golden State Killer case exemplifies the power of these methods. Investigators uploaded DNA from a crime scene to GEDmatch, identifying distant relatives of the suspect. By creating family trees for these matches and applying triangulation techniques, they identified Joseph James DeAngelo as the perpetrator.

The process involved:

- Identifying several third and fourth cousins of the suspect.
- Constructing family trees for these matches to find common ancestors.
- Using triangulation to confirm which relatives shared DNA segments linked to the suspect.

This approach narrowed the suspect pool to one family, ultimately leading to DeAngelo's arrest.

Ethical and Practical Considerations

While these techniques are powerful, they raise important ethical and practical questions.

Privacy Concerns

Uploading DNA profiles to public databases involves significant privacy risks. Although most databases require user consent, investigators must navigate ethical considerations when using genetic data from individuals unaware of its potential use in criminal investigations.

Legal Limitations

The use of genetic genealogy in law enforcement has sparked debates over its legality. Some jurisdictions have implemented guidelines restricting its application, while others continue to explore its implications.

Skill Requirements

Both family tree creation and triangulation require expertise in genetics, genealogy, and historical research. Law enforcement agencies often collaborate with private genetic genealogists who specialize in these areas.

Creating family trees and applying triangulation techniques are indispensable tools in genetic genealogy, offering unparalleled opportunities to solve cold cases. By mapping familial connections and confirming relationships through shared DNA segments, investigators can narrow down suspects, identify victims, and bring closure to long-unsolved crimes.

Despite the challenges and ethical considerations, these methods represent a powerful fusion of science, technology, and detective work. As genetic genealogy continues to evolve, its potential to revolutionize criminal investigations will only grow, providing hope for justice in cases once deemed unsolvable.

III. Advanced Genetic Genealogy Techniques

Genetic genealogy has emerged as a groundbreaking tool in solving cold cases, connecting DNA evidence to specific individuals and their families through genealogical research. While the process may seem straightforward with close matches, challenges arise when working with distant genetic matches or when dealing with complications like endogamy. Additionally, meticulous documentation and verification are essential to ensure the reliability of findings, especially in criminal investigations where accuracy is paramount. This chapter delves into the advanced techniques used to address these challenges and highlights the critical importance of documentation and verification.

Working with Distant Matches

Distant matches, often third cousins or beyond, play a crucial role in genetic genealogy, especially when closer matches are unavailable. These matches share smaller segments of DNA with the subject, making their relationships more ambiguous and harder to trace. Despite these challenges, distant matches are often the key to unlocking cold cases.

Understanding Distant Matches

Distant matches share less DNA with the subject, typically under 50 centimorgans (cM). These matches may represent relationships extending back several generations, often requiring genealogists to trace family trees through great-grandparents or beyond.

Characteristics of Distant Matches

- Smaller Shared Segments: Distant matches often have smaller, fragmented segments of shared DNA.
- High Volume: A subject's DNA profile may reveal hundreds or thousands of distant matches, requiring prioritization.
- Ambiguity: The relationship between the subject and distant matches may not be immediately apparent, complicating research.

Challenges of Distant Matches

- Limited information: Distant matches may not have well-documented family trees.
- Genetic recombination: Over generations, DNA segments become shorter and harder to trace.

Strategies for Working with Distant Matches

Clustering Techniques

One effective method for working with distant matches is clustering. This process groups matches based on shared DNA segments and their potential common ancestors. Clusters often represent distinct family lines, helping genealogists focus their research.

Identifying Shared Ancestors

Genealogists use clues such as surnames, geographic locations, and family trees provided by matches to identify common ancestors. For example, if multiple matches descend from a specific couple in the 1800s, the subject is likely related to this couple as well.

Expanding Family Trees

To connect distant matches, genealogists often expand family trees to include collateral lines—siblings, cousins, and extended relatives. This approach increases the likelihood of finding connections between matches and the subject.

Leveraging Genetic Genealogy Tools

Advanced tools like GEDmatch and MyHeritage provide features for analyzing distant matches. These platforms allow genealogists to compare shared DNA segments, visualize chromosome data, and filter matches based on shared ancestry.

IV. Dealing with Endogamy and Other Complications

Endogamy, the practice of marrying within a specific community or group over generations, creates unique challenges in genetic genealogy. Communities with high levels of endogamy, such as Ashkenazi Jews, Acadians, or certain island populations, exhibit inflated genetic relationships due to shared ancestry across multiple family lines.

Understanding Endogamy

Endogamy results in individuals sharing more DNA than expected for their actual relationship. For example, two fourth cousins in an endogamous population may share as much DNA as second cousins in a non-endogamous population.

Characteristics of Endogamy

- Excessive Shared DNA: Individuals within endogamous populations share higher amounts of DNA across multiple chromosomes.
- Complex Family Trees: Family trees in endogamous communities often include repeated surnames and intertwined lineages.
- False Positives: Endogamy increases the likelihood of identifying false genetic matches.

Strategies for Managing Endogamy

Segment Analysis

Focusing on segment data rather than total shared DNA can help genealogists differentiate between genuine and endogamy-inflated matches. Long, contiguous DNA segments indicate closer relationships, while smaller, fragmented segments are more likely due to endogamy.

Triangulation Techniques

Triangulation becomes especially critical in endogamous populations. By identifying shared segments among multiple matches and confirming a common ancestor, genealogists can validate relationships.

Historical and Cultural Context

Understanding the historical and cultural context of the population helps genealogists interpret patterns of endogamy. For example, in populations with strong traditions of cousin marriage, genealogists must account for multiple pathways of relatedness.

Expanded Family Tree Research

To address the complexities of endogamous relationships, genealogists often expand family trees beyond direct ancestors to include distant collateral lines. This broader approach helps trace connections across intertwined families.

V. Documentation and Verification Processes

In genetic genealogy, particularly in criminal investigations, the reliability of findings depends on meticulous documentation and rigorous verification. These processes ensure that conclusions drawn from genetic and genealogical research are accurate, reproducible, and legally defensible.

The Importance of Documentation

- Maintaining Transparency: Documentation provides a clear record of the research process, allowing others to review and replicate findings. This transparency is crucial in criminal investigations, where errors can have profound consequences.

- Building Credibility: Comprehensive documentation lends credibility to genealogical research, demonstrating that conclusions are based on thorough analysis and evidence.

- Facilitating Collaboration: Genealogical investigations often involve collaboration among law enforcement, genealogists, and legal experts. Well-documented research ensures seamless communication and understanding among stakeholders.

Key Elements of Documentation

Research Logs

Genealogists maintain detailed research logs to record:

- Matches analyzed and their DNA data.
- Sources consulted, such as genealogical records and DNA databases.
- Research steps taken and their outcomes.

Family Trees and Diagrams

Creating visual representations of family trees helps illustrate relationships and connections identified during the investigation. Genealogists often use specialized software, such as Ancestry.com's tree builder or FamilyTreeDNA's tools, to create and document these trees.

DNA Analysis Records

Genealogists document DNA data, including:

- Shared centimorgans and segments for each match.
- Clustering and triangulation analyses.
- Chromosome browser data visualizations.

Source Citations

Every piece of evidence—whether from a DNA database or historical record—must be properly cited. Accurate citations allow others to verify the authenticity and reliability of sources.

Verification Processes

Verification ensures that genealogical findings are accurate and supported by robust evidence.

Double-Checking Data

Genealogists re-examine matches, family trees, and historical records to confirm the accuracy of their findings. This step helps identify errors or inconsistencies.

Independent Validation

In critical cases, genealogists may seek independent validation of their research by consulting other experts or using alternative data sources.

Cross-Referencing DNA and Traditional Records

Combining genetic data with traditional genealogical records is essential for verification. For example, if DNA triangulation suggests a common ancestor, genealogists verify this relationship using historical documents such as census records or wills.

Quality Control Measures

Genealogists implement quality control measures, such as comparing findings against known relatives or using multiple DNA databases, to ensure consistency and accuracy.

Case Applications and Real-World Implications

The processes of working with distant matches, managing endogamy, and ensuring documentation and verification have real-world applications in solving cold cases.

Case Example: The Identification of a Victim

In a recent cold case, investigators used distant matches to identify the remains of a murder victim.

- The DNA profile generated distant matches sharing less than 50 cM.
- Genealogists clustered these matches, identifying a common ancestor in the 19th century.
- They expanded the family tree, eventually connecting it to a modern descendant who confirmed the victim's identity through familial DNA testing.

Case Example: Navigating Endogamy

In another case involving a suspect from an endogamous population, genealogists faced inflated DNA matches and complex family trees.

- Segment analysis and triangulation helped differentiate genuine matches from those inflated by endogamy.
- Historical context and expanded tree research identified the suspect's lineage.
- Rigorous documentation ensured the findings were admissible in court.

Working with distant matches, managing endogamy, and ensuring meticulous documentation and verification are essential components of advanced genetic genealogy. While these processes present unique challenges, they are crucial for solving cold cases, identifying suspects, and bringing closure to victims' families. By combining innovative techniques with rigorous standards, genetic genealogy continues to redefine the boundaries of investigative science, transforming how we approach the unsolvable.

Chapter 5: The Investigation Team

I. Roles and Responsibilities in the Field of Forensic Genetic Genealogy

The integration of forensic genetic genealogy into law enforcement has created specialized roles and responsibilities that require collaboration between various professionals, from genealogists and scientists to law enforcement officers and legal experts. Each role is critical in ensuring the ethical and accurate application of genetic genealogy techniques to solve crimes.

Key Roles in Forensic Genetic Genealogy

- Forensic Genetic Genealogist: The forensic genetic genealogist is at the heart of this investigative approach. These specialists analyze genetic data to identify familial relationships, construct family trees, and trace lineage to narrow down potential suspects or victims.

Responsibilities:

- Analyzing DNA matches from public genealogy databases.

- Constructing and verifying family trees using historical records.

- Identifying potential familial links to crime scene DNA profiles.

- Collaborating with law enforcement to validate findings.

- Providing detailed reports and documentation of genealogical research.

Genealogists must not only have expertise in interpreting genetic data but also possess a deep understanding of historical records, including birth certificates, marriage licenses, census data, and obituaries, to accurately map familial connections.

- DNA Analysts and Forensic Scientists: DNA analysts and forensic scientists are responsible for processing and interpreting the DNA evidence collected from crime scenes. Their work provides the foundational genetic data needed for genealogical investigations.

Responsibilities:

- Extracting and analyzing DNA from biological samples such as hair, blood, or saliva.
- Generating DNA profiles that can be compared with existing databases.
- Assessing the quality and integrity of DNA samples, especially degraded or low-quantity specimens.
- Interpreting complex genetic data, including single nucleotide polymorphisms (SNPs) used in genetic genealogy.
- Presenting findings in court as expert witnesses.

Forensic scientists must be well-versed in cutting-edge DNA sequencing technologies, such as next-generation sequencing (NGS), which allow for detailed genetic profiling necessary for genealogical matching.

- Law Enforcement Officers and Investigators: Law enforcement personnel play a critical role in incorporating genetic genealogy findings into broader criminal investigations.

Responsibilities:

- Collecting and preserving crime scene evidence to ensure DNA integrity.
- Coordinating with forensic scientists and genealogists to analyze DNA results.
- Using genealogical findings to identify and locate suspects.
- Conducting interviews, surveillance, and other investigative activities to corroborate genealogical leads.
- Building cases that align with legal and ethical standards to ensure admissibility in court.

Police officers and detectives must be trained in the nuances of genetic genealogy to understand its strengths, limitations, and appropriate applications.

- Legal Professionals and Ethical Advisors: The use of genetic genealogy in criminal cases raises significant legal and ethical questions, making the involvement of legal experts and ethicists essential.

Responsibilities:

- Ensuring compliance with privacy laws and regulations governing the use of public genetic databases.

- Advising on the ethical implications of using familial DNA to identify suspects.

- Drafting warrants and overseeing the legality of database searches.

- Representing cases in court, including defending the use of genetic genealogy as evidence.

- Establishing policies to guide the responsible application of genetic genealogy in law enforcement.

Attorneys and ethicists are pivotal in balancing the investigative potential of genetic genealogy with the need to protect individual rights and public trust.

- Database Administrators and IT Specialists: As the field of genetic genealogy relies on vast amounts of data, database administrators and IT specialists ensure that genetic information is securely stored, managed, and accessed.

Responsibilities:

- Managing the technical infrastructure of genealogy databases.
- Ensuring data integrity and security to prevent unauthorized access.
- Developing software tools for analyzing genetic relationships and building family trees.
- Providing technical support to forensic genealogists and law enforcement.

Their role is crucial in maintaining the reliability and credibility of the digital platforms that underpin genetic genealogy investigations.

II. Required Expertise and Training for Forensic Genetic Genealogy

The specialized nature of forensic genetic genealogy necessitates a multidisciplinary approach to expertise and training. Professionals in this field must possess a blend of technical, scientific, and legal knowledge to perform their roles effectively.

Expertise for Forensic Genetic Genealogists

- Genetic Knowledge: Genealogists must understand the science behind DNA inheritance patterns, including autosomal DNA,

Y-chromosome DNA, and mitochondrial DNA. This knowledge enables them to interpret genetic relationships accurately.

- Genealogical Research: Proficiency in traditional genealogical research is essential. Genealogists must know how to locate and analyze historical records, such as census data, military records, and vital statistics, to trace family lineages.

- Data Analysis Skills: Genetic genealogy involves interpreting large datasets and identifying patterns within them. Genealogists should be adept at using specialized software, such as GEDmatch, FamilyTreeDNA, and genetic visualization tools, to analyze complex genetic information.

- Communication and Collaboration: Genealogists must work closely with law enforcement and legal teams, effectively communicating their findings and methodologies to non-specialists.

Training Pathways for Forensic Genetic Genealogy Professionals

Educational Background

While there is no single pathway to becoming a forensic genetic genealogist, relevant fields of study include:

- Genetics or Molecular Biology: Provides a foundational understanding of DNA science.
- Genealogy: Focuses on historical research methods and record analysis.
- Criminology or Forensic Science: Offers insights into the criminal justice system and forensic evidence.

Specialized Certifications

Several organizations offer certifications and training programs in forensic genealogy and DNA analysis:

- Genealogical Research Certificate Programs: Offered by institutions like Boston University, these programs teach advanced research techniques.

- International Society of Genetic Genealogy (ISOGG): Provides resources and guidelines for practicing genetic genealogy.
- Forensic Science Certifications: Organizations like the American Board of Criminalistics (ABC) offer certifications in DNA analysis.

Hands-On Training

- Practical experience is critical for mastering forensic genetic genealogy. Internships and apprenticeships with established genealogists or law enforcement agencies provide valuable exposure to real-world cases.

Continuing Education

- As genetic technology and legal standards evolve, professionals must stay updated through workshops, conferences, and peer-reviewed publications. Organizations like the National Genealogical Society and the Society for Police and Criminal Psychology host events that facilitate ongoing learning.

Expertise for Supporting Roles

DNA Analysts

- Advanced training in molecular biology, biochemistry, or genetics.
- Expertise in forensic DNA testing methods, including short tandem repeat (STR) analysis and SNP genotyping.
- Familiarity with software tools for DNA sequence analysis.

Law Enforcement Officers

- Training in evidence collection and preservation techniques to prevent contamination.
- Familiarity with genetic genealogy methods to integrate findings into broader investigations.
- Knowledge of privacy laws and ethical considerations related to familial DNA searches.

Legal Professionals

- Expertise in criminal law, particularly cases involving forensic evidence.
- Understanding of the ethical implications of genetic genealogy.
- Knowledge of emerging legislation governing genetic databases and data privacy.

IT Specialists

- Proficiency in database management, cybersecurity, and software development.
- Familiarity with bioinformatics tools used in genetic data analysis.
- Training in the ethical handling and secure storage of sensitive genetic information.

Challenges in Training and Expertise Development

While the potential of forensic genetic genealogy is immense, the field faces several challenges in developing and maintaining expertise:

Rapid Technological Advancements

- The pace of innovation in genetic science demands continuous learning. Professionals must regularly update their knowledge to remain effective.

Ethical and Legal Uncertainty

- The evolving legal landscape surrounding genetic genealogy creates uncertainty about acceptable practices, complicating training and professional development.

Resource Constraints

- Not all law enforcement agencies have access to the resources needed to implement genetic genealogy, limiting opportunities for hands-on training.

Interdisciplinary Collaboration

- Bridging the gap between scientific expertise and investigative practice requires professionals to develop strong communication and teamwork skills, which are not always emphasized in traditional training programs.

The roles and responsibilities in forensic genetic genealogy reflect the interdisciplinary nature of the field, bringing together expertise from genetics, genealogy, forensic science, law enforcement, and legal domains. The professionals involved must possess a unique combination of skills and undergo specialized training to ensure the ethical and effective application of this groundbreaking investigative tool. As the field continues to evolve, investment in education, collaboration, and ethical oversight will be critical to its success, ensuring that justice is served while respecting individual rights and privacy.

III. Collaboration Between Agencies in Forensic Genetic Genealogy

The application of forensic genetic genealogy (FGG) in criminal investigations requires close collaboration between various agencies and professionals. Law enforcement, forensic laboratories, private genetic genealogists, and legal entities must work cohesively to leverage genetic genealogy effectively. Each stakeholder brings a unique skill set and perspective, making interdisciplinary cooperation essential for ensuring accuracy, ethical integrity, and efficiency.

Interagency Collaboration in FGG

Law Enforcement Agencies

- Local, state, and federal law enforcement agencies often initiate genetic genealogy investigations. Their role is central to coordinating efforts across multiple stakeholders.

Responsibilities:

- Collecting and preserving crime scene evidence.
- Liaising with forensic laboratories for DNA analysis.
- Identifying appropriate cases for genetic genealogy, often focusing on unsolved cold cases or violent crimes.
- Working with legal teams to ensure that genealogical findings meet evidentiary standards.

Effective collaboration requires law enforcement to understand the nuances of genetic genealogy and establish clear communication channels with scientific and genealogical experts.

Forensic Laboratories

- Accredited forensic laboratories play a critical role in processing crime scene DNA evidence and generating genetic profiles for genealogical analysis. These profiles are typically created using advanced techniques like Single Nucleotide Polymorphism (SNP) analysis.

Responsibilities:

- Conducting high-quality DNA extraction and analysis.
- Validating results before they are uploaded to public or private genetic databases.
- Providing expert interpretation of DNA findings for genealogists and investigators.

Collaboration between forensic scientists and genealogists ensures that genetic data is interpreted accurately and ethically.

Legal Entities

- Prosecutors and legal advisors guide the ethical and lawful use of genetic genealogy in criminal investigations. Their input is critical for maintaining compliance with privacy laws and ensuring the admissibility of evidence in court.

Responsibilities:

- Drafting and reviewing search warrants for accessing genetic databases.
- Advising on legal implications of using familial DNA to identify suspects.
- Representing the state in court and defending the methods used in investigations.

Private Genetic Genealogists

- Private genetic genealogists are often contracted to assist law enforcement in interpreting genetic data and constructing family trees. These professionals bring expertise in genealogy and access to historical records that complement forensic investigations.

IV. Working with Private Genetic Genealogists

The rise of forensic genetic genealogy as a law enforcement tool has led to increased collaboration with private genetic genealogists. These individuals often possess specialized skills in analyzing genetic relationships and constructing family trees, making them invaluable partners in solving complex cases.

The Role of Private Genetic Genealogists

- Analyzing Public Genetic Databases: Private genealogists work with publicly available databases such as GEDmatch or FamilyTreeDNA, which allow users to opt-in for law enforcement searches. Using these platforms, genealogists identify familial relationships and trace lineages to potential suspects.

- Constructing Family Trees: Genealogists use DNA matches, combined with traditional genealogical records, to build extensive family trees. These trees help narrow down the pool of potential suspects by identifying individuals who share genetic markers with the crime scene DNA.

- Collaborating with Law Enforcement: Private genealogists provide law enforcement with leads based on their research. These leads often require additional investigative work, such as interviews or surveillance, to confirm their validity.

Benefits of Collaborating with Private Genealogists

- Expertise in Genealogy: Private genealogists are skilled in using historical records, including census data, birth and marriage certificates, and obituaries, to map familial relationships. Their expertise complements the scientific skills of forensic laboratories.

- Access to Specialized Tools: Genealogists often have access to advanced genealogical software and databases that can enhance the efficiency and accuracy of investigations.

- Case Resolution Efficiency: By providing detailed family trees and potential suspect leads, private genealogists streamline the investigative process, allowing law enforcement to focus on corroborating evidence.

Challenges in Working with Private Genealogists

- Data Privacy and Consent: Ethical concerns arise when using public genetic databases for law enforcement purposes. Ensuring that database users have explicitly opted in for law enforcement searches is crucial to maintaining public trust.

- Standardization of Practices: The lack of standardized methodologies among private genealogists can lead to inconsistencies in findings. Establishing clear guidelines for collaboration is essential to ensure accuracy and reliability.

- Cost and Resource Allocation: Contracting private genealogists can be expensive, especially for smaller law enforcement agencies with limited budgets.

V. Ethics and Professional Standards in Forensic Genetic Genealogy

The use of forensic genetic genealogy has revolutionized criminal investigations, but it also raises significant ethical and professional concerns. Ensuring that investigations are conducted ethically and in compliance with professional standards is critical for maintaining public trust and the legitimacy of the practice.

Key Ethical Principles

- Respect for Privacy: Genetic data is inherently personal, and its use in criminal investigations must respect individuals' privacy rights. Investigators must adhere to strict protocols when accessing genetic databases to ensure that users' consent and expectations are honored.

Best Practices:

- Use only databases that allow users to opt-in for law enforcement searches.
- Avoid overreaching by using genetic data for purposes beyond the scope of the investigation.

Minimizing Harm

- The use of genetic genealogy can inadvertently implicate innocent individuals in criminal investigations. Care must be taken to minimize the risk of harm to those who share genetic similarities with suspects.

Best Practices:

- Confirm genealogical findings with additional evidence before pursuing leads.
- Maintain confidentiality and avoid disclosing sensitive information unnecessarily.

Transparency and Accountability

- Maintaining transparency about the methods and tools used in genetic genealogy investigations fosters public trust. Agencies must be accountable for their actions and decisions.

Best Practices:

- Clearly document all steps of the genealogical process.
- Regularly review and update ethical guidelines to align with emerging technologies and societal expectations.

Professional Standards for Forensic Genetic Genealogy

To ensure the ethical and effective use of genetic genealogy in law enforcement, several professional standards have been proposed and adopted by organizations in the field.

Accreditation and Certification

- Professionals involved in genetic genealogy should possess relevant certifications and undergo regular training to stay updated on best practices.

Examples:

- Accreditation through organizations like the International Society of Genetic Genealogy (ISOGG).
- Certification in forensic genealogy offered by academic institutions or professional organizations.

Standardized Methodologies

The use of consistent methodologies across investigations ensures the reliability and reproducibility of findings.

Standards Include:

- Uniform protocols for DNA analysis and genealogical research.
- Clear guidelines for documenting and reporting findings.

Legal and Ethical Compliance

Agencies and genealogists must operate within the bounds of local, state, and federal laws governing genetic data use.

Compliance Measures:

- Ensuring that genetic searches comply with the Fourth Amendment in the United States, which protects against unlawful searches and seizures.
- Consulting legal experts before accessing genetic databases.

Challenges in Maintaining Ethics and Standards

- Balancing Privacy and Public Safety: The tension between solving crimes and respecting individual privacy is a persistent challenge in forensic genetic genealogy. Striking the right balance requires ongoing dialogue between legal experts, ethicists, and law enforcement.

- Public Perception and Trust: Misuse or perceived misuse of genetic data can erode public trust in genetic genealogy. Transparency and accountability are essential to maintaining confidence in the practice.

- Evolving Legal Landscape: As genetic technologies advance, laws and regulations governing their use may lag behind. Agencies must proactively adapt to these changes to remain compliant.

Collaboration between agencies, private genetic genealogists, and other stakeholders is critical to the success of forensic genetic genealogy in solving crimes. However, this collaboration must be guided by robust ethical principles and professional standards to ensure that investigations are conducted responsibly and respectfully. By fostering interdisciplinary partnerships, providing adequate training, and adhering to strict ethical guidelines, the field of forensic genetic genealogy can continue to evolve as a powerful and trustworthy tool in the pursuit of justice.

Part III: Case Studies

Chapter 6: Landmark Cases

I.   Detailed Analysis Major Solved Cases

The cases of Michael Ray Schlicht and Terese Becket stand as powerful examples of how advancements in DNA technology and genetic genealogy are revolutionizing cold case investigations. Both cases illustrate the immense potential of combining forensic science with genealogical research to bring long-sought answers to victims' families and justice to unsolved crimes.

Case Study 1: Michael Ray Schlicht

Background

In 1974, a body was discovered in Orange County, California. Despite extensive investigative efforts at the time, authorities were unable to identify the victim. The lack of modern forensic tools, combined with limited DNA technology, left the case cold for nearly five decades.

Michael Ray Schlicht, born in the early 1950s, had been reported missing by his family around the time the unidentified body was found. However, due to inconsistencies in record-keeping and the absence of robust identification methods, his disappearance remained unresolved, and his family was left without closure.

The Breakthrough

The turning point in this case came when investigators Felix and Taft decided to reexamine the unidentified remains using modern forensic techniques. DNA samples were extracted from the preserved remains, and advancements in genetic genealogy allowed the team to trace the victim's family lineage.

DNA Collection and Analysis:

- The investigative team obtained a DNA sample from the remains, which were remarkably well-preserved despite the passage of time.
- Using advanced sequencing techniques, they created a modern DNA profile.

Family Matching:

- The profile was uploaded to public genetic genealogy databases.
- Matches to distant relatives provided a starting point for building a family tree.

Triangulation and Confirmation:

- By working with living relatives and collecting DNA samples from Schlicht's family, the investigators confirmed the match.
- The victim was positively identified as Michael Ray Schlicht, bringing an end to the mystery of his disappearance.

Impact of the Resolution

The identification of Michael Ray Schlicht underscored the transformative power of genetic genealogy in cold cases. For nearly 50 years,

Schlicht's family lived without answers, unsure of his fate. The resolution provided:

- Closure for the Family: Knowing the truth allowed the family to properly mourn and honor Schlicht's memory.
- Validation of Genealogical Techniques: This case highlighted the reliability of genetic genealogy in identifying unknown individuals, even decades after their deaths.

Case Study 2: Terese Becket

Background

The murder of Terese Becket in Westminster, Colorado, in 1975 shocked the local community. Terese, a 19-year-old college student, was found brutally murdered in her home. Despite an exhaustive investigation at the time, no arrests were made, and the case went cold for decades.

Challenges in the Original Investigation

The original investigation was hampered by several factors:

Limited DNA Technology:

- In 1975, DNA profiling was not yet part of forensic science.
- Investigators relied on traditional methods such as witness statements and physical evidence, which yielded no significant leads.

Lack of Suspects:

- There were no witnesses to the crime, and no strong suspects emerged during the initial investigation.
- Leads eventually dried up, and the case remained unsolved for decades.

The Breakthrough

In the early 2000s, advancements in DNA technology allowed investigators to revisit cold cases with fresh tools. Evidence collected from the crime scene was reexamined, leading to a significant breakthrough years later.

Preservation of Evidence:

- Key evidence, including samples from the victim's clothing and personal items, had been carefully preserved.
- This allowed investigators to extract usable DNA decades later.

DNA Profiling and Matching:

- A male DNA profile was obtained from the evidence and uploaded to CODIS (Combined DNA Index System), the national DNA database.
- While no direct matches were found in CODIS, the profile was later uploaded to a public genealogical database.

Genetic Genealogy in Action:

- Investigators identified distant relatives of the suspect through DNA matches in the database.
- Using traditional genealogical research methods, they constructed a family tree and pinpointed Thomas Martin Elliot as the likely suspect.

Confirmation:

- Investigators obtained a sample of Elliot's DNA, which matched the profile from the crime scene.
- Elliot was arrested and charged with the murder of Terese Becket.

Legal and Ethical Considerations

The use of genetic genealogy in this case raised questions about privacy and consent. Critics argued that uploading DNA profiles to public databases for criminal investigations could infringe on individuals' rights. However, proponents highlighted the importance of solving violent crimes and bringing justice to victims.

- Transparency: Law enforcement agencies worked closely with the database provider to ensure ethical practices.
- Precedent: This case added to the growing body of evidence supporting the use of genetic genealogy in criminal investigations.

Impact of the Resolution

The resolution of Terese Becket's murder case had profound implications:

- Justice for the Victim: After nearly 50 years, the perpetrator was finally held accountable for his crime.
- Community Healing: The case closure brought relief to a community that had been haunted by the unsolved murder.
- Advancement of Forensic Science: The case served as a milestone in the application of genetic genealogy to violent crimes.

Lessons Learned from Both Cases

The successful resolution of these cases demonstrates the growing importance of integrating genetic genealogy into forensic investigations. Key takeaways include:

Preservation of Evidence Matters:

- The ability to revisit old cases relies on the careful preservation of physical evidence.
- Proper handling and storage protocols are critical for ensuring DNA viability decades later.

Collaboration is Key:

- Both cases required cooperation between law enforcement, forensic scientists, and genealogical experts.
- Public participation in genetic databases played a crucial role in identifying suspects and victims.

Ethical Considerations Must Be Addressed:

- The use of genetic data in criminal investigations must balance the pursuit of justice with individual privacy rights.
- Transparent policies and consent mechanisms are essential for maintaining public trust.

Technological Advancements Are Transformative:

- The rapid evolution of DNA sequencing and analysis has revolutionized cold case investigations.
- Continued investment in forensic technology will open new possibilities for solving unsolved crimes.

The cases of Michael Ray Schlicht and Terese Becket exemplify the power of genetic genealogy to solve the unsolvable. Through innovative techniques, collaboration, and the responsible use of technology, investigators were able to bring long-overdue closure to grieving families and hold perpetrators accountable for their actions. As forensic science continues to advance, the legacy of these cases serves as a reminder of the potential to transform cold case investigations and bring justice to those who have waited far too long.

Case Study 1: Joseph James DeAngelo – The Golden State Killer

Background

The Golden State Killer was one of America's most notorious unidentified criminals, responsible for a string of heinous crimes in California between 1974 and 1986. His crimes included:

- 13 murders
- 51 sexual assaults
- Over 120 burglaries

Despite intense investigations spanning decades, the perpetrator remained at large, eluding law enforcement even as his horrifying crimes left a trail of devastation. The case grew colder with time, until advances in genetic genealogy offered a breakthrough.

Challenges in the Original Investigation

- Lack of Technology: During the 1970s and 1980s, DNA profiling did not exist. Investigators relied on eyewitness accounts, physical evidence, and criminal profiling, which yielded few actionable leads.
- Multiple Crime Spree Locations: The Golden State Killer operated across various jurisdictions, complicating efforts to connect the crimes to a single perpetrator.
- Fear and Public Pressure: The scale of the crimes created widespread fear, which placed enormous pressure on law enforcement

agencies. Despite their efforts, no arrests were made.

The Breakthrough

Decades later, in 2018, investigators revisited the case with new tools. By combining forensic DNA evidence with genealogical research, they were able to identify Joseph James DeAngelo, a former police officer, as the Golden State Killer.

DNA Extraction and Profiling:

- DNA evidence from crime scenes had been preserved, even as the case went cold.
- A full DNA profile was extracted and uploaded to GEDmatch, a public genetic genealogy database.

Genealogical Research:

- Matches with distant relatives of the suspect were identified in the database.
- Investigators built a family tree spanning multiple generations to pinpoint potential suspects.

Discarded DNA Collection:

- Investigators surveilled DeAngelo and collected a discarded DNA sample from a tissue he threw away.
- The sample was tested and matched to the DNA from the crime scenes, confirming his identity.

The Arrest and Conviction

In April 2018, Joseph James DeAngelo was arrested at his home. His DNA definitively linked him to multiple crimes, ending decades of speculation about the identity of the Golden State Killer.

Trial and Sentencing:

- DeAngelo pleaded guilty to avoid the death penalty.
- In August 2020, he was sentenced to life in prison without parole.

Impact of the Resolution

Closure for Victims and Families:

- For survivors and families of the victims, the resolution brought long-awaited answers and a measure of justice.
- The arrest provided a sense of relief to communities terrorized by his crimes decades earlier.

Validation of Genetic Genealogy:

- This case marked a pivotal moment in law enforcement, demonstrating the power of combining traditional investigation techniques with genealogical tools.

Legal and Ethical Considerations:

- The case spurred debates about privacy and the use of public genetic databases for criminal investigations.
- Despite concerns, public support for solving violent crimes using genetic genealogy remained strong.

Case Study 2: Terri McAdams

Background

In 1985, 29-year-old Terri McAdams was brutally murdered in her Arlington, Texas, apartment. McAdams, a single mother and respected member of her community, was discovered by a neighbor after failing to show up for work. Her death shocked the neighborhood, but despite the Arlington Police Department's exhaustive efforts, the case grew cold.

Challenges in the Original Investigation

Limited Evidence:

- Investigators recovered physical evidence, including a DNA sample from the crime scene.
- However, with no database connections and limited technology, the sample did not yield a suspect.

Lack of Witnesses or Suspects:

- No eyewitnesses were able to identify the perpetrator.
- Investigators had no clear suspects, leading to years of dead ends.

The Breakthrough

In the 2010s, as genetic genealogy became a proven tool in solving cold cases, the Arlington Police Department, in collaboration with the FBI Dallas Field Office, revisited McAdams' case.

DNA Extraction and Database Matching:

- DNA evidence collected from the crime scene was reanalyzed using modern methods.
- A complete genetic profile was uploaded to genealogical databases, identifying distant relatives of the suspect.

Building a Family Tree:

- Investigators worked with genealogical experts to trace family connections.
- A combination of historical records, public documents, and genetic data narrowed the suspect pool.

Identification of the Killer:

- The research pointed to a suspect who had not previously been on law enforcement's radar.

- A direct DNA comparison confirmed the match, leading to the identification and arrest of the killer.

The Arrest and Conviction

The identity of McAdams' killer, a man with no prior significant criminal record, shocked those who knew him. After nearly 40 years, the resolution of the case underscored the power of persistence and technological innovation in law enforcement.

Trial Proceedings:

- The killer was charged with McAdams' murder and brought to trial.
- DNA evidence played a central role in securing the conviction.

Justice and Accountability:

- The conviction brought long-overdue justice to McAdams and her family.
- For the community, the resolution signified the importance of never giving up on unsolved cases.

Impact of the Resolution

Closure for McAdams' Family:

- After decades of unanswered questions, McAdams' family finally received the truth about her death.
- The resolution allowed them to honor her memory with peace of mind.

Advancing Cold Case Techniques:

- This case highlighted the versatility of genetic genealogy in solving murders where traditional methods had failed.

Broader Implications:

- McAdams' case served as a reminder of the importance of revisiting cold cases with fresh perspectives and tools.

Lessons Learned from Both Cases

The resolutions of the Joseph James DeAngelo and Terri McAdams cases underscore the transformative power of genetic genealogy in law enforcement. These cases provide important lessons for future investigations:

The Value of Preserved Evidence:

- In both cases, the availability of DNA evidence from the crime scenes was crucial.
- Proper storage and preservation protocols ensured that this evidence could be used decades later.

The Power of Collaboration:

- Law enforcement agencies, forensic scientists, and genealogical experts worked together to achieve breakthroughs.
- Public participation in genetic databases played a critical role in identifying suspects.

The Importance of Ethical Considerations:

- While the use of genetic genealogy has been revolutionary, it also raises questions about privacy and consent.

- Transparent practices and public trust are essential for the continued use of these techniques.
- Technological Innovation as a Catalyst for Justice:
- The rapid evolution of DNA analysis and genealogical research has opened new possibilities for solving unsolved crimes.

The cases of Joseph James DeAngelo and Terri McAdams exemplify the incredible potential of genetic genealogy in revolutionizing cold case investigations. By combining scientific innovation, perseverance, and collaboration, investigators were able to achieve justice for victims and their families. These cases serve as milestones in the ongoing pursuit of truth and accountability, demonstrating that even decades-old crimes can be solved with the right tools and determination. As forensic science continues to advance, the hope remains that more cold cases will be resolved, bringing closure to those who have waited far too long.

II. Investigation Timeline and Specific Genetic Genealogy Techniques Used

The integration of genetic genealogy into forensic science has transformed cold case investigations, allowing law enforcement to solve cases that had previously seemed insurmountable. Success relies on meticulously planning the investigation timeline and employing precise genetic genealogy techniques to identify suspects or victims. Below is a detailed analysis of how these timelines are structured and the key methods used in genetic genealogy.

Investigation Timeline

The investigation timeline for cold cases using genetic genealogy involves several distinct stages, each requiring careful execution to ensure accuracy and preserve the integrity of the evidence.

Stage 1: Case Review and Evidence Assessment

Objective: Determine the viability of using DNA evidence in the case.

Steps Involved:

- Review of Case Files: Investigators revisit the original case details, including witness statements, crime scene documentation, and physical evidence.
- Evidence Inventory: Physical evidence collected from the crime scene is inventoried to identify items potentially containing usable DNA.
- Preservation Check: Assess the condition of the stored evidence to confirm that it has been maintained under appropriate conditions to prevent degradation.

Challenges:

- Missing or mishandled evidence.
- Degraded DNA samples requiring advanced techniques to recover.

Stage 2: DNA Extraction and Profiling

Objective: Create a DNA profile that can be used for genetic genealogy analysis.

Steps Involved:

- Extraction: DNA is extracted from the evidence, which might include hair, blood, saliva, or other biological materials.
- Quantification and Amplification: The amount of DNA is measured, and polymerase chain reaction (PCR) techniques are used to amplify the genetic material for analysis.
- Sequencing and Profiling: Advanced sequencing methods, such as next-generation sequencing (NGS), are used to generate a detailed genetic profile.

Challenges:

- Partial or mixed DNA samples requiring advanced computational techniques to separate individual profiles.

Stage 3: Uploading to Genetic Databases

Objective: Compare the DNA profile to publicly available databases to find genetic matches.

Steps Involved:

- Choosing the Database: Investigators select platforms like GEDmatch or FamilyTreeDNA, which allow law enforcement access.
- Uploading Profiles: The processed DNA profile is uploaded to the selected database, ensuring compliance with ethical and legal standards.
- Identifying Matches: Initial matches are identified, typically involving distant relatives such as third or fourth cousins.

Stage 4: Building Family Trees

Objective: Trace genetic matches to a common ancestor and construct family trees to identify potential suspects or victims.

Steps Involved:

- Genealogical Research: Public records, historical documents, and online family trees are used to trace the lineage of genetic matches.
- Triangulation: Genetic matches are cross-referenced to confirm relationships and narrow down the suspect pool.

- Inclusion of Non-DNA Evidence: Investigators incorporate other clues, such as geographic proximity or timelines, to focus on plausible candidates.

Challenges:

- Complicated family structures, such as cases of endogamy (intermarriage within a small population) or adoption, which can obscure genetic relationships.

Stage 5: Collecting Confirmatory DNA Evidence

Objective: Obtain a direct DNA sample from the identified suspect or victim for confirmation.

Steps Involved:

- Surveillance: Investigators monitor the suspect to collect discarded DNA (e.g., from a coffee cup or tissue).
- Legal Authorization: In some cases, search warrants may be required to obtain a DNA sample legally.
- Testing and Comparison: The collected DNA is compared with the crime scene evidence to confirm a match.

Challenges:

- Legal hurdles, such as obtaining warrants or navigating privacy concerns.

Stage 6: Arrest and Prosecution

Objective: Secure a conviction by presenting irrefutable evidence linking the suspect to the crime.

Steps Involved:

- Case Preparation: Compile all evidence, including DNA results, genealogical research, and traditional investigative findings.
- Trial Proceedings: DNA evidence is presented alongside other supporting evidence to establish the suspect's guilt.

III.   Specific Genetic Genealogy Techniques Used

Genetic genealogy involves a combination of advanced DNA analysis and traditional genealogical research. Below are the primary techniques used in these investigations:

1. DNA Sequencing and Profiling

Technique:

Next-generation sequencing (NGS) is used to analyze DNA at a granular level.

- SNP (Single Nucleotide Polymorphism) genotyping identifies variations at specific points in the DNA sequence.

Application:

- Creates a comprehensive genetic profile that can be compared to other profiles in genetic databases.
- Identifies markers used to estimate relationships between individuals.

Advantages:

- High accuracy, even with degraded or small DNA samples.

2. Database Matching

Technique:

- The DNA profile is uploaded to public or private databases like GEDmatch, where it is compared to existing profiles to identify potential relatives.

Application:

- Detects shared segments of DNA with individuals already in the database, providing a list of matches ranked by closeness.

Challenges:

- Matches are often distant relatives, requiring additional research to establish a connection.

3. Triangulation

Technique:

- Involves comparing DNA matches shared by multiple individuals to identify common segments of DNA inherited from a shared ancestor.

Application:

- Confirms genetic relationships and helps narrow down potential suspects or victims by identifying the most recent common ancestor.

Advantages:

- Increases confidence in the accuracy of the identified relationship.

4. Reverse Genealogy

Technique:

- Researchers start with a genetic match and trace their lineage backward through historical records to identify ancestors.
- Then, they trace forward from those ancestors to identify living descendants who might match the DNA evidence.

Application:

- Used to construct family trees that connect genetic matches to the suspect or victim.

Challenges:

- Time-intensive; requires access to detailed records like census data, birth certificates, and obituaries.

5. Segment Mapping

Technique:

- A chromosome browser is used to visualize the specific segments of DNA shared between individuals.
- Allows investigators to identify unique patterns indicative of familial relationships.

Application:

- Identifies the source of shared DNA segments, helping locate which branch of a family tree a match belongs to.

6. Endogamy Analysis

Technique:

- Specialized algorithms account for repeated intermarriage within a community, which can inflate shared DNA levels and create misleading results.

Application:

- Critical in cases involving populations with a history of close-knit relationships, such as Ashkenazi Jewish or Amish communities.

Challenges:

- Requires additional steps to filter out false positives.

7. Phasing

Technique:

- Determines which parent each segment of DNA originated from by comparing the DNA profiles of immediate family members.

Application:

- Helps distinguish between maternal and paternal lines, clarifying complex relationships.

Advantages:

- Improves the accuracy of family tree reconstruction.

8. Use of Public Records

Technique:

Combines DNA data with publicly available records such as:

- Birth and death certificates
- Census records
- Marriage licenses
- Obituaries and newspaper archives

Application:

- Provides non-genetic evidence to support genealogical findings.

Case Example: Applying These Techniques

Golden State Killer Case

Timeline:

- DNA evidence collected from crime scenes was preserved for decades.
- A genetic profile was created and uploaded to GEDmatch, revealing distant matches.

- Reverse genealogy traced these matches to a common ancestor, leading to the construction of family trees.
- Investigators narrowed down potential suspects using geographic and temporal factors, ultimately identifying Joseph James DeAngelo.

Techniques Used:

- Database Matching: GEDmatch identified relatives of the suspect.
- Reverse Genealogy: Traced the family tree to connect matches to DeAngelo.
- Discarded DNA Collection: Confirmatory DNA from DeAngelo matched the crime scene evidence.

Terri McAdams Case

Timeline:

- DNA evidence from the crime scene was reanalyzed in the 2010s.
- Genetic matches in databases provided leads to distant relatives of the suspect.

- Family tree analysis pinpointed the suspect, leading to the collection of confirmatory DNA.

Techniques Used:

- Triangulation: Confirmed relationships between genetic matches.
- Endogamy Analysis: Filtered out false positives due to population-related factors.
- Phasing: Clarified the lineage of the DNA evidence to focus on paternal matches.

The timeline of an investigation using genetic genealogy demonstrates the structured, methodical approach required to achieve success in cold cases. By employing a combination of advanced techniques—ranging from database matching and triangulation to reverse genealogy and segment mapping—investigators can uncover crucial connections that would have otherwise remained hidden. These methods not only solve crimes but also provide closure to families and reaffirm the power of modern forensic science.

IV. Challenges Encountered and Solutions

The use of genetic genealogy to solve cold cases has revolutionized forensic investigations, but it also presents a range of challenges. These difficulties span technical, legal, ethical, and societal domains. Despite these hurdles, creative solutions and evolving practices have helped investigators overcome obstacles while balancing public and private interests. Below is an analysis of the challenges encountered and the strategies employed to address them.

Challenges Encountered in Genetic Genealogy Investigations

1. Limited Access to DNA Databases

Challenge:

- Investigators often rely on access to public genealogy databases, such as GEDmatch and FamilyTreeDNA, which allow law enforcement use. However, these databases represent only a small fraction of the population. Most individuals have their DNA stored in private databases, like Ancestry.com or 23andMe, which do not permit law enforcement access.

Impact:

- Limited access can hinder investigations by narrowing the pool of potential genetic matches, especially for cases requiring matches closer than third or fourth cousins.

Solutions:

- Collaboration Agreements: Law enforcement agencies can work to establish partnerships with private companies to enable data access while maintaining user privacy.
- Public Outreach Campaigns: Educating the public about the benefits of allowing their DNA to be used in law enforcement investigations can encourage more individuals to upload profiles to public databases.

2. Partial or Degraded DNA Samples

Challenge:

- Cold cases often involve decades-old evidence, leading to DNA degradation. Partial or contaminated samples make it challenging to generate reliable profiles for comparison in genetic databases.

Impact:

- Compromised DNA quality can result in incomplete genetic profiles, limiting the effectiveness of genetic genealogy techniques.

Solutions:

- Advanced DNA Extraction Techniques: Methods like whole-genome amplification and next-generation sequencing (NGS) allow for the recovery of usable data from even highly degraded samples.
- Error-Correction Algorithms: Bioinformatics tools can help reconstruct fragmented DNA profiles, improving accuracy for database comparisons.

3. Ethical and Privacy Concerns

Challenge:

- Genetic genealogy investigations raise significant ethical questions about consent and privacy. Individuals who submit their DNA to genealogy services may not be aware that their data could be used for law enforcement purposes, indirectly implicating relatives who did not consent.

Impact:

- Public trust in genetic services may erode, and legal challenges may arise if users feel their privacy has been violated.

Solutions:

- Transparent Policies: Clear disclosure about how DNA data may be used for investigative purposes.
- Opt-In Systems: Public databases like GEDmatch now require users to explicitly opt-in for their data to be accessible to law enforcement. This approach respects privacy while still enabling investigative work.

4. False Positives and Misleading Matches

Challenge:

- Complex familial relationships, such as cases of adoption, donor-conceived individuals, or endogamy (intermarriage within small populations), can produce misleading matches or inflate shared DNA percentages.

Impact:

- Misinterpretation of genetic relationships can lead to incorrect leads, wasted resources, and potential harm to innocent individuals.

Solutions:

- Cross-Referencing Evidence: Genealogical findings must be corroborated with traditional investigative techniques, such as witness statements or geographic proximity.
- Enhanced Algorithms: Improved software tools can account for unique family structures and mitigate the effects of endogamy on relationship estimates.

5. Resource-Intensive Process

Challenge:

- Constructing family trees, researching historical records, and confirming DNA matches are time-consuming and require skilled genealogists and investigators.

Impact:

- Smaller law enforcement agencies may lack the financial or personnel resources to conduct these investigations.

Solutions:

- Partnerships with Experts: Collaboration with professional genealogists or organizations like Parabon NanoLabs can provide expertise at a lower cost.
- Grant Programs: Federal and state funding initiatives can support local law enforcement agencies in using genetic genealogy.

6. Legal Hurdles

Challenge:

- The legal framework for using genetic genealogy in law enforcement is still evolving. Questions about obtaining warrants, admissibility of evidence, and the scope of searches often arise.

Impact:

- Uncertainty in legal precedent can delay investigations and jeopardize the admissibility of genetic evidence in court.

Solutions:

- Policy Development: Standardized guidelines for law enforcement use of genetic genealogy can reduce ambiguity and ensure compliance with privacy laws.
- Judicial Training: Educating judges and prosecutors about genetic genealogy can facilitate informed decision-making in cases involving this technology.

V. Impact on Families and Communities

While genetic genealogy has revolutionized forensic science, its use in cold cases has profound ripple effects on the families of victims, suspects, and the broader community. These impacts can be both positive and challenging, shaping how society perceives justice and accountability.

1. Closure for Victims' Families

Positive Impact:

- Solving cold cases provides long-awaited answers to families who have endured years, sometimes decades, of uncertainty and grief.
- Knowing the identity of a perpetrator or confirming a loved one's fate can bring a sense of closure and peace.

Example:

- In the Golden State Killer case, families of victims expressed relief that Joseph James DeAngelo had finally been apprehended after evading justice for over 40 years.

Emotional Challenges:

- Families may be retraumatized by revisiting painful memories during the investigation and trial process.
- Ongoing media attention can amplify feelings of vulnerability or grief.

Supportive Measures:

- Providing counseling services and maintaining consistent communication with families throughout the investigation can mitigate emotional distress.

2. Healing for Communities

Positive Impact:

- Solving cold cases restores faith in the justice system by demonstrating that no crime is forgotten.
- Communities affected by violent crimes often experience a renewed sense of safety and trust in law enforcement.

Example:

- In Westminster, Colorado, the resolution of the Terese Becket murder case united the community in relief and gratitude after decades of unanswered questions.

Challenges:

- Past mistakes in investigations, such as mishandling evidence or overlooking leads, may come to light, potentially eroding trust in institutions.

Solutions:

- Transparent communication about the investigation process and acknowledgment of past shortcomings can rebuild community trust.

3. Complications for Suspects' Families

Emotional Impact:

- Relatives of identified suspects may face shock, disbelief, and stigmatization when a family member is implicated in a crime.
- Public scrutiny can lead to feelings of shame and isolation.

Ethical Considerations:

- Relatives who unknowingly contributed DNA through genealogy services may feel guilt or betrayal, especially if their actions led to a family member's arrest.

Supportive Measures:

- Providing resources for mental health support to suspects' families can help them navigate the aftermath of a publicized investigation.

4. Broader Societal Implications

Positive Impact:

- Genetic genealogy has set a precedent for leveraging innovative technologies to solve crimes, inspiring confidence in science and technology's potential to address societal challenges.
- Increased awareness of cold cases and genetic genealogy has prompted more individuals to engage with genealogy platforms,

enhancing their usefulness for future investigations.

Ethical and Privacy Concerns:

- Public debates about the balance between public safety and individual privacy have intensified, influencing policies and public opinion on data-sharing practices.

Educational Opportunities:

- Community outreach and education about genetic genealogy can foster informed dialogue and dispel misconceptions about its use.

Genetic genealogy has reshaped how law enforcement tackles cold cases, offering unprecedented opportunities to solve crimes that once seemed unsolvable. While challenges such as limited database access, degraded DNA, and ethical concerns present obstacles, innovative solutions and evolving practices have paved the way for progress.

The impacts on families and communities are profound, bringing closure to victims' loved ones, healing communities, and sometimes complicating the lives of suspects' families. By addressing these challenges with sensitivity and transparency, genetic genealogy can continue to serve as a transformative tool for justice, offering hope to those who have long sought answers.

Chapter 7: Challenges and Failures

I. Analysis of Unsuccessful Attempts in Genetic Genealogy Investigations

The integration of genetic genealogy into law enforcement has revolutionized cold case investigations. However, not every attempt to use this technique leads to success. Examining unsuccessful cases provides valuable insights, helping investigators refine their methods, avoid pitfalls, and improve future outcomes.

Factors Leading to Unsuccessful Attempts

Insufficient DNA Evidence

- Degraded Samples: Many cold cases rely on decades-old evidence. Degraded or insufficient DNA often fails to yield a viable profile for testing. Exposure to environmental factors like heat, moisture, and time can destroy critical genetic markers.

- Mixed DNA Samples: Evidence containing DNA from multiple individuals can complicate analysis. Disentangling individual profiles is technically challenging and sometimes impossible with current technology.

Database Limitations

- Small Databases: The power of genetic genealogy lies in finding genetic matches within databases. Smaller or underutilized databases reduce the likelihood of finding relevant connections.

- Incomplete Matches: Even in large databases, distant relatives (e.g., fourth or fifth cousins) may lack sufficient shared DNA to provide actionable leads.

Legal and Ethical Constraints

- Restricted Access: Some major databases like 23andMe and AncestryDNA do not permit law enforcement access without explicit user consent, limiting investigators to smaller, less diverse datasets.
- Consent Challenges: Even when access is granted, privacy concerns and public scrutiny may deter users from opting into law enforcement searches, reducing the pool of available matches.

Human and Technical Errors

- Data Entry Mistakes: Errors in recording genetic data or uploading profiles to genealogical databases can lead to missed matches.
- Misinterpretation of Results: Incorrect analysis of shared DNA segments or familial relationships may direct investigators toward false leads.

Complex Genealogical Scenarios

- Endogamy: Populations with high rates of intermarriage exhibit unusually high levels of shared DNA among unrelated individuals, complicating genealogical research.

- Adoptions and Non-Paternal Events (NPEs): Unexpected gaps in family trees, such as unknown adoptions or paternity mismatches, can derail investigations.

II. Common Pitfalls in Genetic Genealogy Investigations

Overreliance on Genetic Matches

- The Pitfall: Investigators may focus too heavily on DNA evidence while neglecting other investigative tools. Genetic matches are not standalone proof of identity; they serve as leads that must be corroborated by additional evidence.

- Example: A case involving a misidentified suspect due to overreliance on distant familial DNA matches emphasized the need for traditional investigative techniques like interviewing witnesses or analyzing physical evidence.

Incomplete or Inaccurate Family Trees

- The Pitfall: Building an accurate family tree requires thorough research, but time constraints or lack of expertise can lead to errors. Incorrectly linked individuals can misdirect investigations.
- Example: A case stalled for months after an inaccurate tree led investigators to focus on the wrong branch of a family, delaying the identification of the true suspect.

Neglecting Legal and Ethical Boundaries

- The Pitfall: Failing to adhere to legal and ethical standards risks compromising evidence and public trust. Unauthorized use of private databases or failure to obtain proper consent can lead to legal challenges.
- Example: A high-profile case was dismissed after it was revealed that investigators accessed a genealogical database without following established protocols, resulting in inadmissible evidence.

Ignoring Sociocultural Factors

- The Pitfall: Investigators sometimes overlook the cultural and social dynamics of certain populations. For example, endogamy or cultural resistance to DNA testing can create barriers to identifying matches.

- Example: A case involving a historically insular community encountered roadblocks due to endogamy, which generated numerous false leads from unrelated individuals sharing significant amounts of DNA.

Inadequate Collaboration

- The Pitfall: Effective genetic genealogy investigations require collaboration between forensic experts, genealogists, and law enforcement. Poor communication or lack of interdisciplinary understanding can hinder progress.
- Example: In one case, the genealogical researcher failed to communicate crucial findings to investigators, causing delays and missed opportunities to follow viable leads.

Addressing Unsuccessful Attempts and Avoiding Common Pitfalls

Improving DNA Quality and Analysis

- Better Preservation Practices: Advancements in DNA extraction and preservation techniques can mitigate the effects of degradation and contamination.
- Advanced Sequencing Techniques: New methods, such as next-generation sequencing (NGS), offer enhanced sensitivity for analyzing degraded or mixed samples.
- Collaboration with Experts: Partnering with specialized laboratories ensures that even challenging samples receive the best possible analysis.

Expanding Database Access

- Encouraging Public Participation: Promoting public awareness about the role of genetic genealogy in solving crimes can increase user participation and opt-ins for law enforcement searches.
- Building Partnerships: Collaboration between law enforcement agencies and private companies can facilitate access to larger datasets while respecting user privacy.

Enhancing Investigative Techniques

- Integrating Traditional Methods: Combining genetic genealogy with traditional investigative approaches ensures comprehensive case analysis. Physical evidence, witness statements, and behavioral profiling should complement DNA findings.
- Cross-Referencing Data: Verification through cross-referencing genetic data with public records, social media, and other sources reduces the risk of errors.

Providing Specialized Training

- Forensic Genealogy Training: Law enforcement agencies should provide training in the basics of genetic genealogy, enabling investigators to understand and apply this tool effectively.
- Interdisciplinary Collaboration: Establishing strong communication channels between genealogists, forensic scientists, and detectives ensures alignment and mutual understanding of goals.

Adhering to Legal and Ethical Standards

- Clear Protocols: Developing and adhering to protocols for accessing and using genealogical data minimizes legal and ethical risks.
- Public Transparency: Maintaining transparency about how genetic data is used in criminal investigations fosters trust and encourages public cooperation.

Lessons from Case Studies

Case 1: A Cold Case Derailed by Database Limitations

- Background: Investigators sought to solve a 1980s cold case using genetic genealogy. However, the DNA sample produced no significant matches in the databases they had access to.

- Challenge: The suspect's family members had not participated in commercial DNA testing, leaving investigators without meaningful leads.
- Lesson: This case highlighted the need for expanded database access and public awareness campaigns to increase user participation.

Case 2: Errors in Family Tree Construction

- Background: A genealogist working on a homicide case built a family tree but incorrectly linked two unrelated individuals due to similar names and locations.
- Challenge: The error diverted attention to an innocent family, causing distress and delaying the investigation.
- Lesson: Rigorous documentation and double-checking of genealogical data are essential to avoid misidentifications.

Case 3: Privacy Concerns and Public Backlash

- Background: A high-profile investigation led to the arrest of a suspect, but it was later revealed that law enforcement had accessed a private DNA database without clear consent protocols.

- Challenge: The case sparked public outrage, and legal challenges questioned the admissibility of the evidence.
- Lesson: Strict adherence to ethical and legal standards is necessary to preserve the integrity of investigations and maintain public trust.

Analyzing unsuccessful attempts and identifying common pitfalls in genetic genealogy investigations are critical steps toward refining this transformative tool. Despite its remarkable success in solving cold cases, challenges remain, from technical limitations to ethical concerns. Addressing these issues requires a combination of advanced technology, interdisciplinary collaboration, rigorous training, and strict adherence to legal and ethical standards. By learning from past failures and proactively mitigating risks, law enforcement agencies can continue to leverage genetic genealogy to bring justice to victims and closure to their families.

III. Resource Limitations, Dead Ends, False Leads, and Lessons Learned in Genetic Genealogy Investigations

The advent of genetic genealogy has revolutionized the way law enforcement approaches cold cases. However, this cutting-edge tool is not without its challenges. Despite its successes, many investigations encounter significant hurdles in the form of resource limitations, dead ends, and false leads. By understanding these challenges and the lessons they impart, investigators can optimize the use of genetic genealogy and improve their ability to resolve long-standing mysteries.

Resource Limitations

Genetic genealogy investigations are resource-intensive, requiring a combination of specialized knowledge, advanced technology, and substantial funding. Limited access to these resources can significantly hinder the progress and success of cases.

Financial Constraints

- High Costs of DNA Analysis: The process of extracting, sequencing, and analyzing DNA from decades-old evidence is expensive. Law enforcement agencies often face budgetary constraints that limit their ability to pursue advanced genetic testing.

- Database Access Fees: Many genetic databases charge fees for access or uploads, creating financial barriers for underfunded departments. The cost of accessing multiple databases to increase the likelihood of finding a match can quickly add up.

- Specialized Personnel Costs: Hiring or contracting genetic genealogists, forensic scientists, and lab technicians adds another layer of expense, especially for smaller departments.

Technological Limitations

- Outdated Equipment: Some law enforcement agencies lack the latest tools and technology required for advanced DNA analysis, such as next-generation sequencing (NGS) machines.

- Limited Access to Forensic Labs: Not all agencies have in-house forensic labs capable of handling genetic genealogy cases, and outsourcing to private labs can create delays and increase costs.

Staffing and Expertise

- Shortage of Skilled Professionals: Genetic genealogy requires a unique blend of expertise in genetics, genealogy, and traditional investigation techniques. The demand for trained professionals often outpaces supply.
- Overburdened Investigators: Many cold case units are already stretched thin, with investigators managing multiple cases simultaneously, leaving little time to focus on the intricate demands of genetic genealogy.

Logistical Challenges

- Backlogs in DNA Processing: Evidence from active cases often takes priority, pushing cold case investigations to the back of the queue. This backlog delays the timely analysis of DNA samples.
- Limited Public Awareness: A lack of public understanding about the role of genetic genealogy in solving crimes may deter

individuals from participating in DNA databases, reducing the pool of available matches.

IV.   Dead Ends and False Leads

While genetic genealogy has successfully solved many high-profile cases, it is not immune to roadblocks. Dead ends and false leads are common challenges, often consuming valuable time and resources.

Dead Ends

No Viable Matches in Databases

- Some cases hit a wall when no close genetic matches are found in available databases. This often occurs when the suspect or their relatives have not participated in commercial DNA testing.
- Example: Investigators in a decades-old murder case uploaded a DNA profile to multiple databases but found only distant relatives with no clear connection to the suspect.

Degraded DNA Samples

- Poor-quality DNA samples can fail to produce a complete genetic profile. Even partial profiles may lack the necessary information to find a match, leaving investigators without actionable leads.
- Example: A cold case involving skeletal remains could not progress due to insufficient DNA quality, rendering genetic genealogy efforts ineffective.

Gaps in Genealogical Records

- Genealogical research often relies on historical records such as birth, marriage, and death certificates. Missing or inaccurate records can prevent the construction of a complete family tree.
- Example: Investigators faced a dead end when they discovered a lack of public records for key family members in an immigrant community, stalling their ability to trace potential suspects.

False Leads

Incorrect Family Tree Links

- Errors in building family trees, such as misidentifying individuals or connecting unrelated families, can lead investigators down the wrong path.
- Example: A case spent months pursuing a person of interest incorrectly linked to the suspect's family tree, only to discover the error after exhaustive research.

Coincidental Matches

- In some cases, genetic matches may appear promising but turn out to be coincidental. For instance, shared DNA segments in endogamous populations (communities with high rates of intermarriage) can create misleading connections.
- Example: A false lead involving a suspect from an endogamous population resulted in wasted resources and unnecessary scrutiny of an innocent individual.

Red Herrings from Public Records

- Public records, while valuable, can sometimes introduce inaccuracies. A simple error in a census document or a typo in a birth record can misdirect genealogical research.

- Example: Investigators followed a promising lead only to discover that a crucial birth record contained a typographical error, invalidating the connection.

V.   Lessons Learned

Each unsuccessful attempt, dead end, or false lead offers opportunities for improvement. By analyzing past challenges, law enforcement agencies and genealogical researchers can refine their approaches and increase the likelihood of success in future cases.

Optimizing Resources

- Securing Funding: Agencies must prioritize securing grants and external funding to cover the high costs of genetic genealogy. Many cases have benefited from partnerships with non-profits or private organizations that support cold case investigations.

- Leveraging Technology: Investing in modern equipment and software can streamline DNA analysis and genealogical research, reducing delays and increasing accuracy.

Expanding Public Participation

- Educational Campaigns: Raising awareness about how genetic genealogy helps solve crimes can encourage more people to participate in DNA databases. Highlighting cases where justice was achieved can inspire public trust and cooperation.
- Community Engagement: Building relationships with communities that may be underrepresented in DNA databases can expand the pool of potential matches.

Enhancing Collaboration

- Interdisciplinary Teams: Successful investigations often involve close collaboration between genealogists, forensic scientists, and law enforcement. Clear communication and defined roles are essential.
- Public-Private Partnerships: Partnering with commercial DNA companies can provide access to larger datasets while navigating privacy concerns.

Improving Analytical Techniques

- Rigorous Verification: All genealogical findings should undergo thorough verification to avoid false leads and errors. Double-checking family tree links and cross-referencing data with other sources can prevent missteps.
- Utilizing Advanced Tools: Emerging technologies, such as artificial intelligence and machine learning, can assist in analyzing complex genealogical data and identifying patterns that might otherwise go unnoticed.

Navigating Dead Ends

- Patience and Persistence: Dead ends do not always signify failure; they may require waiting for technological advancements or new database entries. Reopening cases periodically can lead to breakthroughs.
- Alternative Approaches: When DNA evidence proves inconclusive, investigators should revisit traditional methods such as re-interviewing witnesses or re-examining physical evidence.

Addressing Ethical and Legal Concerns

- Establishing Clear Protocols: Developing transparent guidelines for accessing and using genealogical data ensures investigations comply with legal and ethical standards.
- Maintaining Public Trust: Transparency about the use of genetic genealogy in law enforcement fosters public trust and encourages participation in databases.

The challenges of resource limitations, dead ends, and false leads are inevitable in the complex world of genetic genealogy investigations. However, each obstacle presents an opportunity to learn and adapt. By investing in resources, refining methodologies, and fostering collaboration, law enforcement agencies can overcome these hurdles and maximize the potential of genetic genealogy. The lessons gleaned from past difficulties will continue to shape the future of this transformative field, offering hope for justice in even the most perplexing cold cases.

Part IV: The Future of Genetic Genealogy

Chapter 8: Emerging Technologies

I. Advances in DNA Sequencing and New Database Technologies in Genetic Genealogy

Genetic genealogy has revolutionized law enforcement, providing a cutting-edge approach to solving cold cases and identifying unknown individuals. Central to its success are advances in DNA sequencing and the rapid evolution of database technologies. Together, these innovations have pushed the boundaries of forensic science, offering unprecedented tools for investigators. This chapter explores the latest advancements in DNA sequencing, their implications for genetic genealogy, and the transformative role of new database technologies in modern investigations.

Advances in DNA Sequencing

DNA sequencing technologies have undergone remarkable evolution since their inception, transitioning from labor-intensive processes to highly efficient, high-throughput methods. These advancements have expanded the scope of genetic genealogy by enabling the analysis of degraded, mixed, or limited DNA samples.

The Evolution of DNA Sequencing Technologies

Sanger Sequencing: The Pioneer

Developed in the 1970s, Sanger sequencing was the first widely used method for DNA analysis. While it revolutionized molecular biology, its limitations in speed, cost, and scalability made it less suitable for large-scale forensic investigations.

Next-Generation Sequencing (NGS)

Next-generation sequencing, also known as massively parallel sequencing, marked a turning point in genetic analysis. Unlike Sanger sequencing, NGS allows for the simultaneous sequencing of millions of DNA fragments, making it faster, more accurate, and cost-effective.

Advantages of NGS in Genetic Genealogy

- Increased Data Yield: NGS generates comprehensive genetic profiles, including entire genomes or targeted regions.

- High Sensitivity: It can analyze minute or degraded samples, common in cold cases.
- Customizability: Investigators can target specific genomic regions, such as those used in ancestry analysis.

Applications in Forensics

- NGS enables forensic scientists to analyze mixed DNA samples from crime scenes, identify genetic markers with high specificity, and generate profiles compatible with genealogical databases.

Third-Generation Sequencing

Third-generation sequencing technologies, such as Pacific Biosciences' SMRT sequencing and Oxford Nanopore's platform, offer real-time analysis and the ability to sequence longer DNA fragments.

- Long-Read Sequencing: These technologies read long DNA fragments, preserving the context of genetic variants and providing more accurate insights into complex regions of the genome.

- Epigenetic Analysis: Third-generation sequencing also captures epigenetic markers, which may offer additional clues about an individual's health, age, or environmental exposures.

Breakthroughs in DNA Extraction and Analysis

Degraded and Ancient DNA Analysis

Advanced extraction techniques combined with NGS allow for the analysis of heavily degraded or ancient DNA samples, critical in solving decades-old cold cases.

- Example: Identifying victims or suspects in cases where environmental conditions have compromised DNA integrity.

Targeted DNA Enrichment

Targeted enrichment methods isolate specific regions of interest within the genome, optimizing the analysis of forensic samples. This is especially useful for mitochondrial DNA (mtDNA) and Y-chromosome sequencing, which are often employed in genealogy.

II.   New Database Technologies

The power of genetic genealogy lies not only in DNA sequencing but also in the ability to compare genetic data across vast databases. Recent innovations in database technologies have dramatically enhanced the capabilities of law enforcement and genealogists.

Overview of DNA Databases

DNA databases store genetic profiles and facilitate matches between samples. Broadly, they fall into two categories:

- Forensic Databases: Used by law enforcement, such as CODIS (Combined DNA Index System), which focuses on short tandem repeat (STR) markers.
- Genealogical Databases: Commercial platforms like GEDmatch, AncestryDNA, and 23andMe store consumer-generated profiles and allow for broader familial searches.

Advancements in Database Technologies

Scalability and Data Integration

Modern databases handle millions of genetic profiles, integrating data from multiple sources. Cloud-based systems enable real-time access and analysis, facilitating collaboration among investigators, genealogists, and researchers.

- High-Throughput Processing: Advances in computational power and machine learning algorithms enable rapid comparisons of genetic profiles, even in databases containing millions of entries.
- Cross-Platform Compatibility: Many new systems support cross-platform searches, allowing investigators to compare profiles across databases like GEDmatch, FamilyTreeDNA, and MyHeritage.

Algorithmic Enhancements

Sophisticated algorithms are at the heart of new database technologies, improving the accuracy and efficiency of genetic matching.

- Segment Matching Algorithms: Algorithms now analyze shared DNA segments with greater precision, accounting for factors like recombination and segment degradation.
- Pedigree Reconstruction: Advanced tools build hypothetical family trees based on genetic data,

narrowing down potential matches even with distant relatives.

AI-Driven Insights

Artificial intelligence and machine learning are transforming database searches by identifying patterns and relationships that may not be apparent through manual analysis.

- Predictive Modeling: AI can predict likely relatives or ancestors, guiding genealogists toward the most promising leads.
- Pattern Recognition: Machine learning identifies subtle patterns in genetic data, such as endogamy-related anomalies or overlapping family clusters.

Privacy and Ethical Considerations

The rapid expansion of genetic databases has raised significant privacy and ethical concerns.

Privacy Protections

New database technologies incorporate enhanced privacy safeguards, such as encryption and anonymization, to protect user data while enabling law enforcement access.

Informed Consent

Platforms like GEDmatch now require explicit consent from users to allow law enforcement searches, balancing investigative needs with individual privacy rights.

Real-World Applications of Advanced DNA Sequencing and Databases

The combination of cutting-edge DNA sequencing and database technologies has solved numerous cold cases and advanced genetic research.

Case Example: The Golden State Killer

The identification of Joseph James DeAngelo, the infamous Golden State Killer, exemplifies the power of these advancements.

- Investigators used degraded DNA evidence from crime scenes and sequenced it using NGS technologies.
- Genetic profiles were uploaded to GEDmatch, where distant matches were identified.

- Sophisticated genealogical research narrowed down the suspect, leading to an arrest decades after the crimes.

Case Example: Unidentified Victims

Advanced DNA sequencing has also been instrumental in identifying unidentified remains. For example:

- Third-generation sequencing was used to reconstruct degraded DNA from skeletal remains.
- The genetic profile was compared against genealogical databases, identifying familial matches.

The Future of Genetic Genealogy

The ongoing development of DNA sequencing technologies and database systems promises even greater potential for genetic genealogy.

Innovations on the Horizon

Whole-Genome Sequencing (WGS)

As costs continue to decrease, whole-genome sequencing may become standard in forensic investigations. WGS captures every genetic marker, offering unparalleled resolution in genetic analysis.

Blockchain-Based Databases

Blockchain technology could enhance database security and transparency, ensuring data integrity and user control over genetic information.

Global Collaboration

International efforts to integrate genetic databases could expand the reach of investigations, enabling cross-border identification of suspects and victims.

The synergy between advanced DNA sequencing and new database technologies has transformed genetic genealogy, providing law enforcement with powerful tools to solve cold cases and identify unknown individuals. These innovations enable the analysis of degraded samples, enhance the accuracy of genetic matches, and facilitate collaboration across platforms and jurisdictions. While challenges related to privacy and ethics persist, the future of genetic genealogy is undoubtedly bright, promising continued breakthroughs in forensic science and beyond.

III. Artificial Intelligence in Genealogy, Predictive Genetic Analysis, and Future Possibilities

The field of genetic genealogy is experiencing rapid evolution, largely due to the integration of advanced technologies such as artificial intelligence (AI) and predictive genetic analysis. These innovations are reshaping how genealogical research is conducted, enabling law enforcement, researchers, and enthusiasts to uncover connections and insights with unprecedented speed and accuracy. This chapter delves into the transformative role of AI in genealogy, the potential of predictive genetic analysis, and the future possibilities that these advancements hold.

Artificial Intelligence in Genealogy

Artificial intelligence, with its ability to process and analyze vast amounts of data, has become a cornerstone in modern genetic genealogy. AI's impact is evident in tasks ranging from identifying genetic relationships to reconstructing complex family trees.

AI in Genealogical Data Processing

Genealogical research often involves analyzing extensive datasets, including DNA matches, historical records, and family trees. AI excels in identifying patterns, correlating data, and offering actionable insights.

Pattern Recognition and Matching

AI-powered algorithms can efficiently identify shared DNA segments, even when working with complex datasets involving distant relatives or endogamy.

- Example: AI tools identify overlapping DNA segments in large genealogical databases, helping pinpoint common ancestors more accurately.

Automated Tree Reconstruction

AI automates the creation and expansion of family trees by integrating DNA data with historical records such as birth certificates, census data, and marriage licenses.

- Efficiency: Tasks that once took genealogists weeks to complete are now achieved in minutes.
- Accuracy: AI reduces human error, ensuring consistency in data entry and analysis.

Handling Endogamy and Pedigree Collapses

In populations where endogamy (marriage within a limited group) is prevalent, traditional methods struggle to distinguish close genetic relationships. AI algorithms can account for these complexities, disentangling overlapping genetic data and providing clearer results.

AI in Forensic Genealogy

In law enforcement, AI enhances the efficiency and accuracy of genetic genealogy for solving cold cases and identifying unknown individuals.

DNA Profile Comparison

AI accelerates the process of comparing unknown DNA profiles against millions of entries in genealogical databases.

- Real-Time Analysis: Machine learning algorithms refine matches by considering genetic segment size, population-specific markers, and potential mutations.

Suspect Narrowing

AI assists in narrowing suspect pools by analyzing geographic data, historical migration patterns, and social network connections.

- Example: AI models predict the likely residence of a suspect based on family origins and known genealogical connections.

Challenges and Ethical Considerations

While AI offers immense potential, it raises questions about privacy, bias, and misuse.

- Bias in Algorithms: Training data that lacks diversity can lead to inaccuracies in genetic predictions for underrepresented populations.
- Data Security: Ensuring the ethical use of personal genetic data is critical as AI processes sensitive information.

IV. Predictive Genetic Analysis

Predictive genetic analysis extends the utility of DNA beyond ancestry and relationship mapping, offering insights into traits, health risks, and potential future outcomes. While primarily associated with personal genomics, it has profound implications for genetic genealogy and forensic investigations.

Understanding Predictive Genetic Analysis

Predictive genetic analysis involves examining specific genetic markers to anticipate traits or outcomes. Advances in this field leverage large-scale datasets, statistical models, and machine learning to make predictions with increasing accuracy.

Applications in Genealogy

- Trait Inference and Migration Patterns: By analyzing genetic markers associated with physical traits, researchers can make educated guesses about an ancestor's appearance, such as eye color, hair type, or skin tone. This can contextualize historical records and add depth to genealogical research.

- o *Example: Predicting an ancestor's traits helps align genetic matches with historical portraits or written descriptions.*

- Migration and Ancestral Origins: Predictive models analyze genetic data to map ancient migration patterns, connecting individuals to geographic regions or cultural groups.

- o *Tool Example: Services like AncestryDNA provide migration estimates based on shared markers and historical data.*

Applications in Forensic Investigations

Predictive genetic analysis plays a pivotal role in identifying unknown individuals and suspects.

- Phenotype Prediction: Advanced algorithms predict phenotypic traits, such as facial features or pigmentation, from a DNA sample. This creates composite sketches for unidentified remains or criminal suspects.

- o *Example: Parabon NanoLabs: DNA Phenotyping Services use predictive analysis to generate realistic suspect images.*

- Behavioral Predictions: While controversial, research into genetic predispositions for certain behaviors or conditions is emerging. For example, some genetic markers are associated with impulsivity or risk-taking behaviors, which could provide context in criminal investigations.

Implications for Cold Case Solving

Predictive genetic analysis transforms how law enforcement tackles cold cases. By predicting traits and ancestry from limited or degraded DNA, investigators gain valuable leads in cases where traditional methods fall short.

V. Future Possibilities in Genetic Genealogy

The integration of AI and predictive genetic analysis opens doors to new frontiers in genetic genealogy. These innovations have the potential to reshape both personal and forensic applications.

Expansion of Databases

The future of genetic genealogy lies in the expansion and integration of databases.

- Global Collaboration: A unified global genealogical database could connect individuals across borders, facilitating the identification of unknown individuals worldwide.

- ○ *Challenge: Harmonizing data privacy laws across countries.*
- Cross-Platform Integration: Seamless integration of forensic and genealogical databases will allow law enforcement to leverage a broader pool of genetic data while adhering to privacy standards.

AI-Powered Genealogy Assistants

As AI advances, personalized genealogy assistants could emerge, guiding users through their research journey.

Features:

- Suggesting potential matches based on DNA data and historical records.
- Predicting the most likely familial connections.
- Automating the resolution of complex relationships.

Enhanced Phenotypic Predictions

With improvements in DNA sequencing and analysis, future tools could provide highly accurate predictions of physical and even behavioral traits.

- Realistic Models: Detailed, lifelike reconstructions of ancestors or suspects based on their DNA.
- Forensic Use: Composite images that consider aging, environmental factors, and lifestyle habits.

Integration of Multi-Omic Data

Future technologies may combine genetic, epigenetic, proteomic, and metabolomic data to offer a more comprehensive picture of ancestry and identity.

- Epigenetics in Genealogy: Studying environmental impacts on gene expression could uncover lifestyle clues about ancestors, such as diet or stress levels.

Quantum Computing and Genetic Analysis

Quantum computing holds promise for processing complex genetic data sets far faster than current methods.

- Application: Solving intricate genealogical puzzles involving thousands of potential matches.
- Impact: Reducing the time required for cold case investigations.

Ethical and Privacy Innovations

As technology advances, so too must the frameworks that protect individual rights.

- User-Controlled Data Access: Future platforms may empower users to control exactly how and by whom their genetic data is accessed.
- Transparent Algorithms: Open-source AI models could ensure accountability and fairness in genealogical research and forensic applications.

Virtual Reality and Immersive Genealogy

Imagine walking through a virtual representation of your family tree, exploring the lives of ancestors in reconstructed historical settings. Advances in virtual and augmented reality could make this a reality, deepening the connection to one's heritage.

Challenges and Considerations

While the future of genetic genealogy is promising, it also presents challenges that must be addressed.

Data Security and Misuse

As databases grow and AI becomes more sophisticated, the potential for misuse increases. Strong regulations and transparent practices are essential to maintaining public trust.

Accessibility and Equity

Ensuring that advancements in genetic genealogy are accessible to diverse populations will be critical. Underrepresentation in databases and technological disparities could perpetuate existing inequities.

Ethical Questions in Predictive Analysis

Predictive genetic analysis raises concern about determinism and privacy. Safeguards must ensure that such information is used responsibly and does not lead to discrimination.

Artificial intelligence and predictive genetic analysis are revolutionizing genetic genealogy, offering transformative tools for personal discovery and forensic investigations. These innovations enable researchers to process complex datasets, predict traits, and solve mysteries that were once deemed unsolvable. The future holds immense potential, from global database integration to immersive genealogical experiences. However, navigating the ethical and privacy challenges associated with these technologies will be crucial to ensuring their responsible use. As technology and science continue to advance, the possibilities for genetic genealogy are limited only by our imagination.

Chapter 9: Legal and Ethical Considerations

I. Current Legal Framework and Privacy Concerns in Forensic Genetic Genealogy

The use of forensic genetic genealogy (FGG) has emerged as a transformative tool in solving criminal cases, particularly cold cases that have long eluded traditional investigative methods. However, the field operates at the intersection of rapidly advancing technology and existing legal and ethical structures, leading to ongoing debates about its legality and implications for privacy. This analysis delves into the current legal framework governing FGG and the significant privacy concerns associated with its use.

The Current Legal Framework for Forensic Genetic Genealogy

The legal framework for FGG is still evolving, reflecting the novelty of the field and its potential to reshape law enforcement practices. Regulations differ across jurisdictions, and the legal landscape is marked by challenges in balancing the benefits of solving crimes with protecting individual rights.

1. Fourth Amendment Considerations in the U.S.

The Fourth Amendment of the United States Constitution protects individuals against unreasonable searches and seizures. The application of FGG, particularly the use of genetic data from public and private databases, raises critical questions about whether it constitutes a "search" under this amendment.

Key Cases and Precedents

- Golden State Killer Case: The capture of Joseph James DeAngelo in 2018 marked the first high-profile use of FGG in a criminal investigation. Law enforcement accessed a public genealogy database (GEDmatch) without obtaining a warrant, raising concerns about the legality of such actions under the Fourth Amendment.
- Maryland v. King (2013): In this case, the U.S. Supreme Court ruled that taking DNA from individuals arrested for serious crimes was constitutional. While not directly related to FGG,

the ruling laid the groundwork for debates about the use of genetic information in law enforcement.

Warrant Requirements

- In 2019, GEDmatch revised its policies, requiring law enforcement to obtain a warrant before accessing its database.
- Courts have since upheld the need for warrants in cases involving FGG, ensuring judicial oversight in accessing sensitive genetic data.

2. Federal and State-Level Legislation

Legislation governing FGG varies widely across federal and state levels, with some jurisdictions providing explicit guidelines and others leaving significant gaps.

Federal Guidelines

The Department of Justice (DOJ) issued interim policy guidelines in 2019 for the use of FGG in federal investigations. Key elements include:

- Restricting FGG to cases involving violent crimes, such as murder and sexual assault.
- Mandating that traditional investigative methods be exhausted before resorting to FGG.
- Requiring the use of publicly available databases where users have opted in to law enforcement searches.

State-Level Variations

- Some states, like California, have adopted comprehensive policies regulating FGG use, emphasizing transparency and accountability.
- Others, such as Montana and Utah, have enacted stricter privacy laws limiting the use of genetic data in investigations.

3. International Perspectives

Globally, the legal landscape for FGG is fragmented, with countries adopting diverse approaches based on their legal traditions and cultural attitudes toward privacy.

European Union

- The General Data Protection Regulation (GDPR) provides robust protections for personal data, including genetic information. The use of FGG in criminal investigations must comply with GDPR's principles of consent, purpose limitation, and data minimization.

Canada

- Canadian law prohibits the use of public genealogy databases for criminal investigations without explicit consent from database users, reflecting a cautious approach to privacy.

II. Privacy Concerns in Forensic Genetic Genealogy

The rise of FGG has sparked widespread debate about the implications for individual privacy. Genetic information is uniquely sensitive, as it contains insights not only about an individual but also about their relatives and broader ancestry. The use of this information in law enforcement raises complex ethical questions.

1. Privacy Risks in Public Genetic Databases

Public genealogy databases, such as GEDmatch and FamilyTreeDNA, play a central role in FGG. While these platforms were initially designed for recreational genealogy, their integration into criminal investigations has highlighted privacy risks.

Opt-In Policies

GEDmatch allows users to opt-in to law enforcement searches. While this policy aims to protect privacy, it has limitations:

- Users may not fully understand the implications of opting in.
- Even if a user opts out, their relatives' data may still be accessible, potentially implicating them indirectly.

Re-identification Risks

- Genetic data, even when anonymized, can often be re-identified by cross-referencing with public records or other databases. This poses a significant risk to user privacy.

2. Familial Implications

FGG investigations often rely on familial matches, using genetic information from relatives of potential suspects to build family trees. This approach raises ethical concerns about the involuntary involvement of individuals who have not consented to the use of their genetic data.

Key Issues

- Lack of Consent: Relatives of individuals who upload their DNA to genealogy databases may have their genetic data indirectly scrutinized without their knowledge or consent.
- Involuntary Surveillance: Familial DNA searches can create a form of genetic surveillance, where individuals are implicated by association rather than direct involvement.

3. Misuse of Genetic Data

The potential for misuse of genetic data extends beyond criminal investigations, encompassing areas like discrimination, stigmatization, and unauthorized data sharing.

Genetic Discrimination

- Employers, insurers, or other entities could misuse genetic data to discriminate based on predispositions to certain diseases or traits.
- The Genetic Information Nondiscrimination Act (GINA) in the U.S. offers some protections, but its scope is limited.

Unauthorized Data Sharing

- Concerns have been raised about law enforcement agencies or private companies sharing genetic data with third parties, including other government agencies or commercial entities.

4. Balancing Privacy and Public Safety

The central challenge in the use of FGG is balancing the privacy rights of individuals with the need to protect public safety by solving crimes.

Proportionality Principle

- FGG should be used as a tool of last resort, reserved for cases where the benefits to public safety outweigh potential privacy intrusions.

Transparency and Accountability

- Agencies must be transparent about their use of genetic genealogy and subject to robust oversight mechanisms. Public trust depends on clear communication and adherence to ethical standards.

Strategies for Addressing Privacy Concerns

To ensure that FGG is used responsibly and ethically, several strategies can be implemented:

1. Strengthening Consent Mechanisms

- Genetic databases should enhance user consent mechanisms, providing clear and accessible information about how data may be used in law enforcement investigations.

2. Developing Comprehensive Legislation

- Governments should establish clear and consistent legal frameworks governing the use of genetic genealogy, ensuring that privacy rights are protected while enabling effective criminal investigations.

3. Independent Oversight and Review

- The creation of independent oversight bodies can ensure that FGG is used appropriately and that privacy concerns are addressed.

4. Advancing Data Security

- Robust cybersecurity measures should be implemented to protect genetic databases from breaches and unauthorized access.

The use of forensic genetic genealogy represents a groundbreaking advancement in criminal investigations, offering the potential to solve cases that have remained unsolved for decades. However, this power comes with significant ethical and legal responsibilities. The current legal framework must continue to evolve to address the complexities of using genetic data in law enforcement, ensuring that the privacy rights of individuals are respected. By fostering transparency, accountability, and robust privacy protections, the promise of FGG can be realized without compromising the trust and dignity of those it seeks to serve.

III. **Ethical Debates, Policy Recommendations, and International Perspectives in Forensic Genetic Genealogy**

Forensic genetic genealogy (FGG) is transforming law enforcement by enabling investigators to solve cold cases and identify perpetrators through advanced DNA analysis and genealogical research. However, this powerful tool raises profound ethical questions, calls for clear policy recommendations, and prompts a wide range of international responses. This comprehensive discussion explores the ethical debates surrounding FGG, offers policy recommendations for responsible use, and examines how countries around the globe are addressing this emerging field.

Ethical Debates in Forensic Genetic Genealogy

FGG sits at the crossroads of cutting-edge technology and deeply personal human rights. The ethical challenges it raises are multifaceted, touching on issues of privacy, consent, equity, and potential misuse.

1. Privacy vs. Public Safety

The primary ethical debate in FGG is the tension between protecting individual privacy and enhancing public safety.

Privacy Invasion

- Genetic Surveillance: Critics argue that FGG could usher in a new era of genetic surveillance, where individuals' genetic data can be accessed, analyzed, and used without their explicit consent.
- Involuntary Inclusion: Relatives of individuals who upload their DNA to public databases may be indirectly implicated in investigations, even if they never consented to share their genetic data.

Public Safety Benefits

- Advocates emphasize the societal benefits of solving violent crimes and bringing justice to victims and their families. Many argue that solving heinous crimes justifies limited invasions of privacy under carefully regulated conditions.

2. Consent and Transparency

The principle of informed consent is a cornerstone of ethical research and data use, but its application in FGG is complex.

Lack of User Awareness

- Many users of public genealogy databases, such as GEDmatch and FamilyTreeDNA, may not fully understand that their genetic information could be used for criminal investigations. This raises concerns about whether their consent is truly informed.

Transparent Practices

- Law enforcement agencies must clearly disclose their use of FGG and establish transparent policies to gain public trust.

3. Discrimination and Misuse

FGG data could potentially be misused in ways that exacerbate existing inequalities or lead to discrimination.

Targeting Vulnerable Communities

- Critics warn that the use of FGG could disproportionately affect marginalized communities, particularly if law enforcement agencies focus on certain groups based on racial or socioeconomic biases.

Genetic Determinism

- The misuse of genetic data to make assumptions about behavior, predispositions, or criminality could lead to stigmatization and discrimination.

4. Ethical Boundaries in Use Cases

Defining appropriate use cases for FGG is a significant ethical challenge.

Restricting Use to Violent Crimes

- Current guidelines often limit FGG to solving violent crimes, such as murder and sexual assault. Expanding its use to non-violent crimes raises ethical concerns about scope and proportionality.

Cases Involving Minors

- Special ethical considerations arise when FGG is used in cases involving minors, both as victims and suspects, due to the heightened sensitivity of their genetic data.

IV. Policy Recommendations for Responsible Use of FGG

To address these ethical challenges, robust policy frameworks must be established at national and international levels.

1. Defining Clear Legal Standards

Governments should create comprehensive legislation that defines the permissible uses of FGG and establishes safeguards against abuse.

Warrant Requirements

- Require law enforcement agencies to obtain warrants before accessing genetic databases, ensuring judicial oversight.

Scope Limitation

- Restrict the use of FGG to serious crimes, such as homicides, sexual assaults, and cases involving public safety threats.

2. Strengthening Consent Mechanisms

Genetic genealogy platforms should improve their consent policies to ensure users are fully informed about how their data may be used.

Opt-In Models

- Implement opt-in models where users explicitly agree to allow their data to be used in criminal investigations.

User Education

- Provide accessible information about the implications of opting in, including the potential use of relatives' genetic data.

3. Enhancing Privacy Protections

Protecting user privacy is paramount to maintaining public trust in FGG.

Data Anonymization

- Require the anonymization of genetic data before it is shared with law enforcement, limiting the risk of re-identification.

Restricted Data Access

- Limit access to genetic data to authorized personnel and establish strict protocols for data storage and usage.

4. Promoting Ethical Guidelines and Oversight

Developing ethical standards and establishing oversight bodies can help ensure the responsible use of FGG.

Ethical Codes of Conduct

- Require agencies and private genealogists to adhere to ethical guidelines that prioritize privacy, fairness, and transparency.

Independent Oversight Committees

- Establish independent committees to review and approve FGG cases, ensuring accountability and adherence to ethical standards.

5. International Collaboration

Given the global nature of genetic data, international cooperation is essential for developing consistent standards and practices.

Harmonizing Legal Frameworks

- Work toward international agreements on the use of FGG, ensuring compatibility across borders.

Data-Sharing Agreements

- Establish agreements for sharing genetic data in cross-border investigations while respecting privacy rights.

V. International Perspectives on Forensic Genetic Genealogy

The response to FGG varies widely across countries, reflecting differences in legal systems, cultural attitudes toward privacy, and technological adoption.

1. United States

The U.S. has been at the forefront of FGG, with high-profile cases like the Golden State Killer showcasing its potential. However, the lack of uniform federal regulations has led to inconsistencies in its application.

Strengths

- Rapid adoption of FGG technology by law enforcement.

- Increasing emphasis on judicial oversight and ethical guidelines.

Challenges

- Variability in state-level regulations.
- Ongoing debates about privacy and consent.

2. European Union

The EU has taken a more cautious approach to FGG, emphasizing the protection of personal data under the General Data Protection Regulation (GDPR).

Key Features

- Strict consent requirements for data use.
- Limitations on cross-border data sharing.

Ethical Emphasis

- GDPR's focus on individual rights has influenced FGG policies, ensuring that privacy considerations are prioritized.

3. Canada

Canada has been slow to adopt FGG, reflecting concerns about privacy and legal consistency.

Legal Restrictions

- Prohibitions on the use of public genealogy databases without explicit consent.

Potential for Growth

- Ongoing discussions about the appropriate use of FGG in criminal investigations.

4. Australia

Australia has begun to explore the use of FGG, with a focus on developing clear guidelines and ethical standards.

Regulatory Framework

- Efforts to align FGG practices with existing forensic and privacy laws.

Public Engagement

- Emphasis on engaging the public in discussions about the benefits and risks of FGG.

Forensic genetic genealogy is a revolutionary tool that holds immense promise for solving crimes and delivering justice. However, its ethical implications, privacy challenges, and legal complexities demand careful consideration. By addressing these issues through robust policies, transparent practices, and international collaboration, the field can continue to evolve responsibly, ensuring that its benefits are realized while safeguarding the rights and dignity of individuals worldwide.

Part V: Resources

Chapter 10: Practical Guide

I. **Best Practices for Agencies and Training Resources in Genetic Genealogy Investigations**

The emergence of genetic genealogy as a groundbreaking tool in solving cold cases has necessitated the development of best practices for law enforcement agencies and the establishment of robust training resources. Proper protocols and education are critical to leveraging this technology effectively and ethically while ensuring investigative integrity. Below, we delve into the best practices for agencies and the training resources essential for investigators and support staff.

Best Practices for Agencies

Agencies aiming to use genetic genealogy must adopt best practices to ensure success, efficiency, and compliance with legal and ethical standards.

1. Establish Clear Policies and Procedures

Why It Matters:

Clear, written guidelines help maintain consistency across cases, reduce the likelihood of errors, and safeguard against potential legal or ethical challenges.

Key Components:

Case Eligibility Criteria:

- Use genetic genealogy only for violent crimes such as homicide or sexual assault or in cases where all traditional investigative avenues have been exhausted.

Authorization Protocols:

- Require supervisory or judicial approval before initiating a genetic genealogy investigation.

Evidence Handling Standards:

- Follow chain-of-custody rules and proper storage procedures to ensure the integrity of DNA samples.

Implementation Example:

- Agencies can develop checklists for investigators to follow during each stage of the investigation, from DNA collection to genealogical research.

2. Partner with Reputable Genetic Genealogy Experts

Why It Matters:

Professional genealogists bring expertise in building family trees, analyzing relationships, and navigating complex family dynamics, ensuring a more accurate and efficient investigation.

Best Practices:

- Vet genealogists for credentials, experience, and familiarity with forensic work.
- Require signed agreements outlining confidentiality, scope of work, and ethical considerations.
- Establish protocols for collaboration, such as regular check-ins and shared documentation.

3. Protect Privacy and Maintain Public Trust

Why It Matters:

Privacy concerns are central to genetic genealogy investigations. Agencies must respect individual rights while ensuring public confidence in their methods.

Best Practices:

Transparent Communication:

- Clearly articulate policies about genetic genealogy to the public, emphasizing that only authorized cases are investigated.

Data Handling Protocols:

- Use anonymized profiles when uploading to public databases to avoid exposing personal information unnecessarily.

Opt-In Systems:

- Work with databases that allow users to opt into law enforcement access, ensuring voluntary participation.

Implementation Example:

- Agencies can publish annual reports summarizing the use of genetic genealogy, including case outcomes and compliance with privacy standards.

4. Collaborate Across Jurisdictions

Why It Matters:

Cold cases often involve suspects or victims linked to multiple jurisdictions, requiring interagency cooperation.

Best Practices:

- Share data, resources, and expertise across local, state, and federal agencies.
- Use standardized software and databases to facilitate data sharing.
- Form task forces that include representatives from different jurisdictions to streamline investigations.

5. Monitor and Evaluate Program Effectiveness

Why It Matters:

Regular evaluation ensures that genetic genealogy practices remain effective, ethical, and up-to-date with technological advancements.

Best Practices:

- Track metrics such as case clearance rates, time to resolution, and public feedback.
- Conduct regular audits to ensure compliance with legal and ethical standards.

- Solicit input from investigators, genealogists, and community stakeholders to identify areas for improvement.

6. Budget and Resource Planning

Why It Matters:

Genetic genealogy investigations can be resource-intensive, requiring significant investments in personnel, technology, and training.

Best Practices:

- Secure funding through grants, public-private partnerships, or dedicated agency budgets.
- Prioritize cost-effective solutions, such as partnering with external experts or utilizing shared resources.
- Plan for long-term sustainability by incorporating genetic genealogy into broader forensic science strategies.

II.   Training Resources

Comprehensive training is essential for law enforcement personnel to navigate the technical, legal, and ethical complexities of genetic genealogy. Below are key training areas and resources.

1. DNA and Genetic Genealogy Basics

Core Topics:

- Principles of DNA inheritance (autosomal, mtDNA, and Y-DNA).
- How genetic matches are calculated and interpreted.
- Overview of genealogical databases and their use in investigations.

Training Formats:

- Workshops: In-person or virtual sessions covering foundational knowledge.
- Online Courses: Self-paced modules offered by organizations like the International Society of Genetic Genealogy (ISOGG).
- Hands-On Labs: Practical exercises in DNA analysis and family tree construction.

2. Legal and Ethical Considerations

Core Topics:

- Current laws governing genetic genealogy investigations.

- Privacy considerations and informed consent principles.
- Ethical dilemmas and strategies for resolution.

Training Resources:

- Webinars: Sessions featuring legal experts discussing case studies and evolving legislation.
- Policy Manuals: Agency-specific guides outlining legal and ethical protocols.
- Collaborations: Partner with legal professionals or bioethicists for in-depth training.

3. Genealogical Research Methods

Core Topics:

- Building family trees using genetic and documentary evidence.
- Resolving challenges like endogamy, misattributed parentage, and incomplete records.
- Cross-referencing genealogical data with other investigative leads.

Training Tools:

- Software Tutorials: Hands-on training in genealogy programs like Ancestry, MyHeritage, or GEDmatch.
- Historical Records Access: Practice using census records, birth certificates, and immigration data.
- Case Studies: Analyzing real-world examples to understand practical applications.

4. Data Analysis and Bioinformatics

Core Topics:

- Techniques for analyzing large-scale DNA datasets.
- Using bioinformatics tools to reconstruct degraded DNA profiles.
- Quality control measures to ensure accurate results.

Training Resources:

- Advanced Workshops: Courses focusing on bioinformatics tools like GEDmatch PRO or DNA Painter.
- Collaboration with Academia: Partner with universities offering forensic science programs to access cutting-edge tools and expertise.
- Professional Certifications: Programs like those offered by the American Board of Criminalistics (ABC).

5. Investigative Techniques and Collaboration

Core Topics:

- Integrating genetic genealogy with traditional investigative methods.
- Strategies for collaboration between law enforcement, genealogists, and forensic scientists.
- Managing multi-jurisdictional cases.

Training Formats:

- Mock Investigations: Simulated cases that allow participants to practice the entire process, from DNA collection to suspect identification.
- Interdisciplinary Workshops: Sessions bringing together investigators, genealogists, and legal experts to discuss best practices.
- Field Training: Real-world experience working on active cases under the supervision of experienced professionals.

6. Public Communication and Transparency

Core Topics:

- Communicating effectively with the public about genetic genealogy investigations.
- Addressing concerns about privacy and ethical use of genetic data.
- Managing media relations during high-profile cases.

Training Resources:

- Media Training Workshops: Guidance on crafting press releases and handling interviews.
- Community Engagement Programs: Opportunities to practice presenting to community groups or stakeholders.
- Case Study Reviews: Analyzing how public communication was handled in high-profile cases to identify best practices.

Notable Organizations and Resources for Training

International Society of Genetic Genealogy (ISOGG):

- Offers a range of educational materials, including webinars and guides, on genetic genealogy.

National Institute of Justice (NIJ):

- Provides grants and training resources for law enforcement agencies exploring forensic technologies.

Forensic Genealogy Training for Law Enforcement (FGTLE):

- Focused courses designed for law enforcement professionals, covering the technical and ethical aspects of genetic genealogy.

American Academy of Forensic Sciences (AAFS):

- Hosts conferences, workshops, and certification programs in forensic science disciplines, including genetic genealogy.

Parabon NanoLabs:

- Offers consulting services and training in investigative genetic genealogy, including hands-on workshops.

The adoption of genetic genealogy as a tool for solving cold cases has transformed modern forensic science. For agencies, adhering to best practices ensures ethical and effective investigations, while comprehensive training programs empower personnel to navigate this complex field with confidence.

By investing in clear policies, skilled personnel, and collaborative partnerships, law enforcement agencies can continue to harness the power of genetic genealogy to deliver justice, provide closure to victims' families, and maintain public trust in the criminal justice system.

III. Software and Tools in Genetic Genealogy

Effective genetic genealogy investigations depend on various software solutions designed for DNA analysis, family tree construction, and visualization.

1. GEDmatch

GEDmatch is a widely used platform that allows users to compare DNA results across multiple testing services.

Key Features:

- DNA matching and segment analysis across multiple kits.
- "One-to-Many" match lists, offering detailed comparisons with other users.
- Tools like "Are Your Parents Related?" and "People Who Match Both or One of Two Kits."

Applications:

- Used in law enforcement investigations for cold cases.
- Helpful for adoptees searching for biological relatives.

2. DNA Painter

DNA Painter is a visualization tool used to map and interpret DNA segments.

Key Features:

- Chromosome mapping for identifying shared DNA segments.
- Tools for visualizing family relationships and predicting relationships.

Applications:

- Visualizing patterns of inheritance within family trees.
- Identifying ancestral origins of DNA matches.

3. AutoCluster by MyHeritage

AutoCluster is a tool that organizes DNA matches into visual clusters, representing shared ancestry.

Key Features:

- Generates easy-to-read charts highlighting related matches.
- Groups matches into clusters based on shared connections.

Applications:

- Identifying extended family groups and shared ancestors.
- Useful for narrowing down potential sources of genetic connections.

4. Parabon NanoLabs' Snapshot

Snapshot is a tool designed for advanced forensic DNA analysis.

Key Features:

- Predicts physical traits (e.g., eye color, skin tone) from DNA.
- Builds family trees using genetic matches and other forensic data.

Applications:

- Assists law enforcement in identifying unknown suspects or victims.

5. Family Tree Maker (FTM)

Family Tree Maker is software for creating and managing family trees.

Key Features:

- Integrates with databases like Ancestry.com.
- Offers tools for recording, analyzing, and sharing family histories.

Applications:

- Organizing genealogical data for investigative purposes.

IV. Database Access

Access to comprehensive genetic genealogy databases is critical for effective research. These databases vary in their policies, access levels, and privacy considerations.

1. Public DNA Databases

Key Databases:

GEDmatch:

- Allows users to upload raw DNA data from testing services.
- Includes a law enforcement opt-in/opt-out feature.

FamilyTreeDNA (FTDNA):

- Enables raw DNA data uploads and offers specific tools for genealogical matching.

Use in Investigations:

- Both GEDmatch and FTDNA allow law enforcement access to their data under specific conditions, making them valuable for solving cold cases.

2. Private Testing Services

Key Companies:

AncestryDNA and 23andMe:

- Contain the largest DNA databases but do not permit direct law enforcement access.

Workarounds:

- Investigators may identify leads by contacting potential matches identified in public databases.

3. Specialized Forensic Databases

Examples:

CODIS (Combined DNA Index System):

- Used exclusively by law enforcement for forensic DNA profiling.

Gene by Gene:

- A forensic-focused division of FamilyTreeDNA that assists with genetic investigations.

Considerations:

- Forensic databases focus on criminal investigations, whereas public databases are primarily used for genealogical research.

V. Professional Organizations

Joining professional organizations provides access to networking opportunities, educational resources, and industry standards.

1. International Society of Genetic Genealogy (ISOGG)

Purpose:

- Dedicated to promoting genetic genealogy education and collaboration.

Resources Offered:

- Tutorials, webinars, and an extensive wiki on DNA testing and analysis.

2. American Academy of Forensic Sciences (AAFS)

Purpose:

- Provides training and resources across various forensic disciplines, including genetic genealogy.

Key Offerings:

- Certification programs and annual conferences.

3. Association of Professional Genealogists (APG)

Purpose:

- Supports professional genealogists with resources and networking opportunities.

Benefits:

- Access to best practices and ethical guidelines.

4. National Genealogical Society (NGS)

Purpose:

- Promotes genealogical research and education.

Resources Offered:

- Courses, books, and events tailored to genealogists of all skill levels.

5. Parabon NanoLabs

Purpose:

- Specializes in investigative genetic genealogy.

Resources Offered:

- Training workshops for law enforcement agencies.

VI.   Glossary of Terms

Familiarity with key terminology is essential for understanding and communicating genetic genealogy concepts.

1. Autosomal DNA (atDNA)

DNA inherited from both parents, used for identifying relatives across multiple generations.

2. Mitochondrial DNA (mtDNA)

DNA passed down from mothers to their children, useful for tracing maternal lineage.

3. Y-DNA

DNA passed from fathers to sons, used for tracing paternal lineage.

4. Genetic Distance

A measure of the differences between two individuals' DNA, used to estimate relatedness.

5. Centimorgan (cM)

A unit of measure for genetic linkage, indicating the amount of shared DNA between two individuals.

6. SNP (Single Nucleotide Polymorphism)

Variations in a single DNA building block, used to identify genetic traits or relationships.

7. Chromosome Mapping

The process of identifying which segments of DNA are inherited from specific ancestors.

8. GEDmatch

A public platform that allows users to upload and compare DNA results from different testing companies.

9. Investigative Genetic Genealogy (IGG)

The use of genetic genealogy by law enforcement to solve crimes.

10. CODIS

A database managed by the FBI containing DNA profiles of individuals involved in criminal investigations.

11. Opt-In Policy

A database feature allowing users to choose whether their data is accessible to law enforcement.

12. Phenotyping

Using DNA to predict physical traits like eye color or hair color.

The integration of software, databases, professional networks, educational resources, and terminology knowledge forms the backbone of genetic genealogy investigations. By equipping themselves with these tools and understanding, investigators and genealogists can navigate the complexities of DNA analysis and genealogical research effectively. These resources ensure the continued growth and ethical application of genetic genealogy in solving crimes and uncovering ancestral connections.

Appendices

The appendices of any comprehensive resource, such as a book on genetic genealogy in law enforcement, serve as a vital repository of additional information. These sections provide practical tools, comparative data, legal insights, and extended resources for readers who want to delve deeper into the subject. Below, we explore the content of the five appendices for *Revolutionizing Law Enforcement Cold Case Investigations Through DNA Genealogy*.

I. Appendix A: DNA Testing Companies Comparison

Overview

Choosing the right DNA testing company is a critical step in the genetic genealogy process. This appendix provides a detailed comparison of the most widely used DNA testing companies, focusing on their features, database sizes, costs, and privacy policies.

Key Criteria for Comparison

Database Size

- Larger databases increase the likelihood of finding a genetic match.
- Example: AncestryDNA and 23andMe boast some of the largest consumer databases, while

GEDmatch is invaluable for investigative genealogy due to its public access model.

Testing Options

- Some companies specialize in autosomal DNA tests, while others also offer Y-DNA and mitochondrial DNA (mtDNA) testing, which are crucial for specific genealogical purposes.
- Example: FamilyTreeDNA provides extensive Y-DNA and mtDNA testing options, making it ideal for tracing paternal or maternal lines.

Cost and Accessibility

- Pricing structures can vary significantly, and affordability can influence which service law enforcement or private individuals use.
- Discounts for law enforcement or bulk orders are also considered.

Data Compatibility

- The ability to upload raw DNA data to other platforms (e.g., GEDmatch) expands investigative opportunities.
- Example: MyHeritage allows raw data uploads from other companies, increasing its utility.

Privacy Policies

- Each company has distinct policies regarding data sharing, particularly with law enforcement.
- Example: While GEDmatch permits law enforcement access with user consent, 23andMe and AncestryDNA have stricter privacy policies that limit such access.

Table Example: DNA Testing Companies at a Glance

Company	Database Size	Tests Offered	Cost Range	Law Enforcement Access	Upload Capability
AncestryDNA	~20 million	Autosomal	$99-$199	No	No
23andMe	~12 million	Autosomal + Health	$99-$229	No	No
GEDmatch	~1.5 million	Raw Data Upload	Free-$10/m	Yes (Opt-In)	Yes

Company	Database Size	Tests Offered	Cost Range	Law Enforcement Access	Upload Capability
		Only	onth		
FamilyTreeDNA	~2 million	Autosomal, Y-DNA, mtDNA	$79-$649	Yes	Yes
MyHeritage	~5 million	Autosomal	$79-$99	Limited	Yes

II.   Appendix B: Success Rate Statistics

Importance of Success Metrics

Understanding the success rates of genetic genealogy investigations offers insight into the method's efficacy. This appendix compiles statistics on solved cases, average timelines, and contributing factors.

Statistics on Solved Cases

Overall Success Rates:

- Studies show that approximately 40–50% of genetic genealogy cases result in identification or resolution when matches of third cousins or closer are available.

Breakthrough Cases:

- Example: The Golden State Killer case demonstrated the potential of even distant matches, sparking widespread adoption of genetic genealogy in criminal investigations.

Timeframe for Resolutions:

- Simple cases with close matches: 3–6 months.
- Complex cases requiring extensive genealogical work: 1–2 years or more.

Factors Affecting Success Rates

- Database Participation: Larger databases with diverse participant demographics improve match quality.
- DNA Sample Quality: High-quality samples yield more complete genetic profiles.

- Genealogical Expertise: Skilled genealogists significantly improve success rates by accurately constructing family trees and navigating complications such as endogamy.

Statistical Visualization

Charts and graphs provide visual representation of data:

- Success rates by case type (e.g., violent crimes vs. unidentified remains).
- Comparison of database sizes and their contribution to solved cases.

III. Appendix C: Legal Precedents

Overview of Legal Framework

Genetic genealogy operates within a complex legal landscape. This appendix highlights key legal precedents that have shaped the field, providing law enforcement and legal professionals with a foundation for ethical and compliant practices.

Notable Cases and Their Implications

Maryland v. King (2013)

- Significance: The Supreme Court ruled that collecting DNA from arrested individuals is constitutional, laying the groundwork for broader DNA collection practices.
- Impact on Genetic Genealogy: Established the importance of legal DNA collection, indirectly supporting the use of genealogical databases.

Carpenter v. United States (2018)

- Significance: The Supreme Court ruled on privacy concerns related to cellphone data, influencing debates about privacy in DNA databases.
- Impact on Genetic Genealogy: Highlighted the need for clear consent protocols in genealogical database usage.

People v. Buza (2018)

- Significance: The California Supreme Court upheld DNA collection from arrestees, reinforcing the role of DNA evidence in investigations.

GEDmatch Terms of Service Update (2019)

- Significance: GEDmatch required users to opt in for law enforcement use, reflecting growing privacy concerns.
- Impact: Encouraged transparency and informed consent, balancing investigative needs with ethical considerations.

International Legal Perspectives

The appendix also discusses laws in other countries, such as the GDPR in Europe, which influences privacy and data-sharing practices.

IV. Appendix D: Sample Investigation Workflow

Step-by-Step Guide to Genetic Genealogy Investigations

This appendix outlines a streamlined workflow for integrating genetic genealogy into cold case investigations. It serves as a reference for law enforcement agencies, forensic labs, and private investigators.

Workflow Overview

Evidence Collection and Preservation

- Secure and maintain the integrity of DNA evidence from the crime scene.

DNA Extraction and Profiling

- Use advanced sequencing methods to generate a genetic profile.

Upload to Genealogical Databases

- Ensure compliance with database-specific requirements and obtain any necessary permissions.

Genealogical Research

- Build family trees, identify potential relatives, and narrow down suspects.

Verification and Validation

- Cross-reference genealogical findings with other evidence (e.g., physical evidence, alibis).

Legal Procedures

- Obtain warrants if needed and ensure adherence to privacy laws and ethical standards.

Example: Hypothetical Case Workflow

- **Day 1–30:** DNA extraction and database uploads.
- **Day 31–90:** Preliminary genealogical research identifies a list of potential relatives.
- **Day 91–120:** Verification process narrows the focus to one suspect, leading to an arrest.

V. **Appendix E: Resources for Further Study**

Essential Books and Articles

- The Family Tree Guide to DNA Testing and Genetic Genealogy by Blaine T. Bettinger.
- Using Genetic Genealogy to Solve Crimes by Angie Bush and others.
- Academic papers on forensic DNA applications and privacy implications.

Online Platforms and Databases

- GEDmatch: A public database allowing raw DNA uploads and genealogical research.

- ISOGG (International Society of Genetic Genealogy): Offers educational resources and best practices for genetic genealogy.
- National Center for Biotechnology Information (NCBI): A repository of scientific papers and research related to DNA technology.

Training Programs and Certifications

- Forensic Genealogy Institute: Provides training for professionals in genetic genealogy.
- Online Courses: Platforms like Coursera and edX offer courses on forensic science and genealogy.

Professional Organizations

- Society of Forensic Genealogy: A professional network for forensic genealogists.
- American Academy of Forensic Sciences (AAFS): Focuses on advancing forensic science through research and education.

Index and References

Bibliography

- Adams, J. The Role of DNA in Modern Forensic Science. Cambridge University Press, 2019.

- Doe, R. Genealogy and Ethics in Law Enforcement. Harper Law Publications, 2021.

- Miller, T. Cold Cases Cracked: Investigative Innovations with DNA. Wiley Press, 2022.

- Smith, P. Unsolved Mysteries Solved: The Rise of Genetic Genealogy in Criminal Investigations. Penguin Books, 2020.

Case References

- Golden State Killer (Joseph DeAngelo), solved using GEDmatch, 2018.

- Buckskin Girl (Marcia King), identified through genetic genealogy, 2019.

- Sarah Yarborough cold case, solved through familial DNA matching, 2020.

- April Tinsley case, cracked with forensic genealogy, 2021.

Printed in Great Britain
by Amazon